In Memory Of

Edna I. Schultz
Reading Teacher

THE LIFE HISTORY OF THE UNITED STATES

Volume 2: 1775-1789

THE MAKING OF A NATION

THE ART OF SEWING

THE OLD WEST

THE EMERGENCE OF MAN

THE AMERICAN WILDERNESS

THE TIME-LIFE ENCYCLOPEDIA OF GARDENING

LIFE LIBRARY OF PHOTOGRAPHY

THIS FABULOUS CENTURY

FOODS OF THE WORLD

TIME-LIFE LIBRARY OF AMERICA

TIME-LIFE LIBRARY OF ART

GREAT AGES OF MAN

LIFE SCIENCE LIBRARY

THE LIFE HISTORY OF THE UNITED STATES

TIME READING PROGRAM

LIFE NATURE LIBRARY

LIFE WORLD LIBRARY

FAMILY LIBRARY:

   THE TIME-LIFE BOOK OF THE FAMILY CAR

   THE TIME-LIFE FAMILY LEGAL GUIDE

   THE TIME-LIFE BOOK OF FAMILY FINANCE

THE LIFE HISTORY OF THE UNITED STATES

Consulting Editor, Henry F. Graff

Volume 2: 1775-1789

THE MAKING OF A NATION

by Richard B. Morris

and the Editors of

TIME-LIFE BOOKS

TIME-LIFE BOOKS, NEW YORK

THE AUTHOR of Volumes 1 and 2 in this series, Richard B. Morris, is an outstanding authority on America's colonial period. Dr. Morris is Gouverneur Morris Professor Emeritus of History at Columbia University and has been a visiting professor at various universities from Hawaii to Paris. He is editor of the *Encyclopedia of American History* and of the authorized compilation of the John Jay papers, and co-editor of the *New American Nation* series. He has written many volumes on U.S. history, including *The American Revolution Reconsidered* and *The Peacemakers*, which won the Bancroft Prize in 1966.

THE CONSULTING EDITOR for this series, Henry F. Graff, is Professor of History at Columbia University in New York.

Valuable assistance in the preparation of this book was given by Roger Butterfield, picture consultant to the Editor; photographers Nina Leen, Eliot Elisofon and George Silk; Editorial Production, Norman Airey; Library, Benjamin Lightman; Picture Collection, Doris O'Neil; Photographic Laboratory, George Karas; TIME-LIFE News Service, Murray J. Gart. Revisions Staff: Harold C. Field, Joan Chambers.

CONTENTS

1. THE FIGHTING JOINED

IT was an hour before midnight. Amid the darkened households of slumbering Boston, a pair of lanterns glimmered on the North Church steeple. Across the water, moonlight picked out a file of British Grenadiers and Light Infantry knee-deep in the Cambridge Marsh as they disembarked from small boats. There they stood until 2 a.m., waiting for provisions to be rowed across Back Bay. Resuming their soggy march, the redcoats pushed through waist-deep water on their way to Lexington. Toward that little Massachusetts town others were converging before dawn on April 19, 1775.

The patriot underground in Boston had sent two mounted messengers to spread the alarm. William Dawes, a tanner, hurried across Boston Neck to Cambridge and Lexington, as a well-known engraver and silversmith named Paul Revere was rowed over to Charlestown to spread the news by another route. For the plan of the British to seize the rebel chiefs, Sam Adams and John Hancock, at their headquarters in the outskirts of Boston and to destroy the rebels' military stores at Concord was perhaps the best-publicized secret of the American Revolution. Now the only open question—what route the British would take—was answered ("two if by sea") and the countryside could be warned. Revere roused the captain of the minutemen at Medford and alerted almost every house along the route to Lexington, where he persuaded Hancock and Sam Adams to seek a safer hiding place. The town bell tolled, signal guns boomed, and just before dawn a band of militia and minutemen—70 at the

EQUIPMENT OF WAR, a drum and gleaming rifles reflect the Revolution's martial spirit. The drum bears a face and the banners of France and the North Carolina militia.

very most—muskets in hand, lined up at the north end of Lexington Common. The tramp of feet was soon heard, and out of the morning mist emerged six companies of redcoats under Major John Pitcairn. A British officer on horseback approached the minutemen, swung his sword and, according to one account, shouted: "Lay down your arms, you damned rebels, or you are all dead men!" Captain John Parker, his grandson recounted with eloquence after the fact, charged his minutemen: "Don't fire unless fired upon. But if they want a war let it begin here." Then Parker told his men to disperse and take care of themselves. They began to withdraw, but did not drop their precious muskets. Someone yelled "Fire! By God, fire!" A single pistol shot was answered by a fusillade of musketry. When the smoke cleared, eight of the withdrawing minutemen were dead and 10 were wounded.

Who shouted "Fire" and which side fired first are facts as debatable today as in 1775, but the Americans, who promptly put the onus on the redcoats, won the battle of testimony if they did not hold the field. The Massachusetts Committee of Safety swiftly wrote and dispatched its own version of the fighting to all the colonies and even by fast schooner to England, where the American story of Lexington was printed in newspapers 12 days before the official British dispatches appeared in print.

The British pressed on from Lexington to Concord, but the Americans had gained enough time to hide the larger part of their valuable stores. The redcoats destroyed such munitions as they could find. But by now the countryside was buzzing with minutemen pouring into Concord. The Americans held fast at the North Bridge. Then they counterattacked and drove the exhausted redcoats pell-mell back toward Boston.

In the early afternoon, near Lexington, Hugh, Lord Percy, a brigadier general on General Gage's staff, came to the rescue of the retreating British. Percy's fresh troops, about 1,000 men, provided protection while the panic-stricken soldiers of Pitcairn's command re-formed for the march back to Boston. From ambush behind walls, fences, barns and farmhouses the minutemen continued to fire upon the battered redcoats, whose passage was greeted with jeers and yells of "King Hancock forever!" In all, the British suffered 273 casualties, the rebels 93. For professional soldiers it was humiliation. "Whoever looks upon

FIRST MAJOR FIGHT:
CONCORD, APRIL 1775

The road from peace to war was 32 miles long—from Boston to Concord and back. On April 19, 1775, Gage secretly dispatched some 600 men on this road. But Paul Revere was riding ahead, sounding the alarm. He reached Lexington and roused Sam Adams and John Hancock from their sleep. On the road to Concord a British patrol briefly held him prisoner but a companion, Dr. Samuel Prescott, pushed through. At Lexington the British swept minutemen aside, but from Concord home their road was lined by sharpshooting patriots (heavy arrows) and the war had begun.

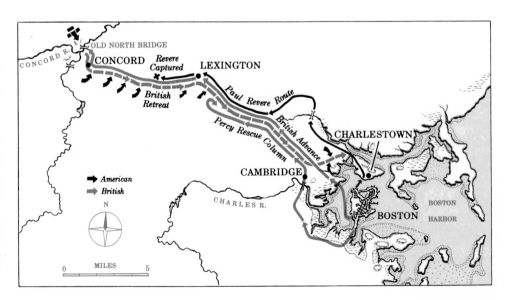

them as an irregular mob will find himself much mistaken," warned Lord Percy. *(See pages 20-21.)*

The war was on. The next day, John Adams brooded: "There's no knowing where our calamities will end." In other states, patriots had already been forewarned. As early as March 23, Patrick Henry told the Virginia Convention, then meeting in defiance of royal orders, that the king was planning to subjugate them. "We must fight," he exhorted. "Gentlemen may cry, 'Peace! peace!' but there is no peace." With marvelous prescience, Patrick Henry added, "The war is actually begun! The next gale that sweeps from the North will bring to our ears the clash of resounding arms." Then, in his memorable peroration, the great orator uttered words that electrified his hearers and quickly received wide circulation: "Is life so dear, or peace so sweet, as to be purchased at the price of chains and slavery? Forbid it, Almighty God! I know not what course others may take; but as for me, give me liberty or give me death!"

When, on the day after Lexington, Virginia's royal governor, Lord Dunmore, ordered marines to seize the militia's gunpowder in Williamsburg, he was menaced by a mob of armed citizens. In retaliation, Dunmore threatened to free the rebels' slaves and burn the town. But he calmed down, paid for the gunpowder and removed it to a naval vessel.

LEXINGTON and Concord transformed a local, political struggle into an all-out affair in which all 13 colonies could join, and produced as if by magic a rebel army composed of New England patriots who flocked to the insurgent encampment outside Boston. Ringing the town from Dorchester to Chelsea, this force cut off Boston from land delivery of needed supplies.

The first rebel army to take the field included such enterprising spirits as Israel Putnam, the bull-necked veteran of the Indian wars who marched his troops from Connecticut; John Stark, the tough New Hampshire backwoodsman and future hero of Bennington; Henry Knox, the Boston bookseller who mastered the artilleryman's trade from books; Nathanael Greene, the fighting Quaker from Rhode Island; and Joseph Warren, the fire-eating Boston physician who exclaimed of some supercilious Britons, "These fellows say we won't fight; by heavens, I hope I shall die up to my knees in blood!" (He got his wish, for he was killed in the battle of Bunker Hill.)

The high-ranking officers at British headquarters in Boston were a rather mixed lot. Thomas Gage, their stodgy commander, received substantial reinforcements on May 25, along with a diverse trio of major generals. One of these, William Howe, was soon to become commander-in-chief. The other two were "Gentleman Johnny" Burgoyne, a dashing wit, playwright and member of Parliament, and Henry Clinton, a complex, extremely cautious man who was unhappy at taking orders from others but who lacked the initiative and nerve for effective command himself.

A menacing prospect confronted Gage. The patriots isolating Boston by land might blow the British fleet right out of the harbor if they could fortify Bunker and Breed's Hills in the Charlestown area or seize Dorchester Heights. On the night of June 16, British fears were realized when some 1,600 patriot troops stole across Charlestown Neck and with pick and shovel dug in on Breed's Hill, the one closest to Boston. British sentries heard the activity, but nobody thought it important enough to disturb Gage. The Royal Navy reacted first, without liaison with Gage. At dawn a naval vessel in the harbor opened

Sir William Howe, six feet tall, handsome and a great connoisseur of good food and pretty women, replaced Gage in the fall of 1775 as British commander-in-chief. Howe won important victories, capturing New York and Philadelphia. But final victory escaped him, and suspicions grew that Sir William was more active in pleasure than war. When he resigned, disheartened, in 1778, all America mockingly sang:

Awake, arouse, Sir Billy,
There's forage in the plain.
Ah, leave your little Filly
And open the campaign.
Heed not a woman's prattle
Which tickles in the ear,
But give the word for battle
And grasp the warlike spear.

fire. At noon, under cover of shellfire from the fleet, Howe's troops were ferried across to the peninsula. Later the ships' guns were turned on snipers firing from Charlestown, nestled at the foot of the hills, soon reducing the town to ashes. In early afternoon Howe moved his 2,200 men forward. The main body was committed to a frontal sweep up Breed's Hill, while Howe himself led a force against the rail fence behind which Colonel William Prescott's men had been stationed to guard the American flank.

Prescott ordered the Americans to hold their fire until the enemy came within 15 to 20 paces. Then the fighting farmers discharged a murderous barrage. Howe's men fled toward their boats, regrouped and, displaying magnificent courage, sallied forth again. Once more they were cut down. Now, reinforced by Clinton, Howe had his men drop their packs and form for a bayonet charge. On this third try they carried Breed's Hill in fierce hand-to-hand fighting with the patriots, who, when their powder ran out, were reduced to using stones—or muskets as clubs. Then the British rapidly assaulted and won Bunker Hill. Putnam's dislodged Americans withdrew in good order, but Howe stopped pursuit at the base of the hill.

Dapper and debonair, 34-year-old Joseph Warren, a wealthy and prominent Boston doctor, fought as an ordinary rifleman in the fierce battle at Bunker Hill and lost his life there. He died, reported one of his British enemies, "in his best. . . . Everybody remembered his fine, silk fringed waistcoat."

WHEN Gage wrote home that the loss "is greater than we can bear," he was not exaggerating the effects of this Pyrrhic victory, for British casualties of 1,054, among them every officer on Howe's personal staff, included 226 dead. For the survivors there were some hard questions. Why had Gage failed to seize Charlestown Neck and thus cut off the Americans from reinforcements? And why had he rushed to attack before trying a naval bombardment? Why had Howe allowed the American forces to withdraw largely intact?

Bunker Hill posed some hard questions for the Americans, too. Why weren't Putnam's men thrown into the breach? Why had only a fraction of the available manpower been used? Why was not more powder sent up to the defenders? These questions pointed to glaring weaknesses in the patriot army: its lack of unified command, its poor discipline, its inadequate arrangements for provisions and supplies. Worst of all, the 16,000 men ringing Boston were a paper army, for most soldiers had enlisted for only a short term, and picked up and left the moment their time was up—sometimes even while fighting was going on. They elected their own officers—and then often refused to obey them. In an emergency, troops "consulted" together, in the manner of a town meeting.

Israel Putnam ("Old Put") was a nearly illiterate farmer whose earlier feats of derring-do in the French and Indian wars won him at 67 a general's rank in Washington's army. He ardently loved a battle—Bunker Hill was mainly Putnam's idea—but as a general, he was more vigorous than wise.

Some of these problems had been foreseen by the Second Continental Congress, which convened at Philadelphia on May 10 and was dominated by more radical spokesmen than the First Congress. Two days before Bunker Hill, John Adams suggested that Congress designate the forces around Boston a Continental Army and that a commanding general be named.

Adams had a strong candidate for this important post. The man he proposed to lead an exclusively northern, small-farmer, town-artisan army was a Southerner, a great landholder and a wealthy aristocrat. But George Washington at 43 was the ablest soldier in the colonies, widely known for his service in the French and Indian wars. He was present as a delegate from Virginia. His wealth gave him influence among other rich men, whose support was badly needed. As a Southerner, he could call on his neighbors to assist the Yankees.

All of these considerations must have been in Adams' mind, and their force was recognized by the unanimous approval given to his motion. Colonel Washington, impressive in his Virginia militia uniform, accepted the appointment on condition that he receive no salary. Then, breaking the news to his wife Martha ("my dear Patsy"), the commander-in-chief confided, "As it has been a kind of destiny that has thrown me upon this service, I shall hope that my undertaking it is designed to answer some good purpose."

Congress then dispatched to Boston 10 rifle companies as reinforcements. Fifteen days after Bunker Hill, Washington reached Cambridge to assume his command, and his influence was quickly felt. He tightened defenses, stiffened discipline, built barracks, accumulated supplies and even pried some money out of a reluctant Congress.

Washington labored to build a real army, first trying to induce the militiamen, many of whose enlistments ended December 31, 1775, to enroll as "Continental" troops for one year, beginning January 1, 1776. But of the host around Boston, only 3,500 signed up. When all save a few of the Connecticut militia departed, Washington angrily wrote: "Such a dirty, mercenary spirit pervades the whole, that I should not be at all surprised at any disaster that may happen." Yet somehow, out of those who stayed, out of fresh recruits and new regiments from the other colonies, Washington created the first American army. It would know many defeats and almost unbelievable hardships. That it stayed together all the way to 1783 is to the credit of the tall, somber, indomitable Virginian who led it.

In the summer of 1775 the great siege of Boston began. The capture of Bunker Hill had secured for Gage the high ground on Charlestown peninsula. But he had never bothered to seize Dorchester Heights, another hill from which cannon could pound the British ships—if the patriots could find the guns. Luckily, the Massachusetts Committee of Safety had learned earlier that British-held Fort Ticonderoga on Lake Champlain had a wealth of artillery and other military stores. The committee appointed a former druggist and merchant to raise a company in western Massachusetts to attack the fort.

THUS arrived on the widening stage of the American Revolution that reckless egoist Benedict Arnold. Daring, ambitious and a nourisher of real or imagined wrongs, he was nonetheless an authentic military genius. But before Arnold could organize his force, Ethan Allen, orotund leader of Vermont's "Green Mountain Boys," was sent on the same mission by his native state of Connecticut. When these two prima donnas met near Ticonderoga (Allen with a few hundred soldiers, Arnold alone, as he was too impatient to await his troops), neither would yield command to the other. So they decided that they would issue orders jointly, and on May 10, 1775, the Americans pounced on the sleeping Ticonderoga garrison. An aroused British officer asked by what authority Allen demanded surrender; the Green Mountain hero is said to have responded with majestic grandiloquence: "In the name of the Great Jehovah and the Continental Congress!" Crown Point to the north was soon seized, and the fort at St. Johns, just across the Canadian border, fell a few days later, opening up the traditional military route to Canada.

Ticonderoga provided the artillery so vital to Washington's plans: by prodigious efforts Henry Knox managed to load nearly 60 cannon, including mortars that weighed a ton, on ox-drawn sledges and bring them over rivers and mountains to the siege of Boston in early '76. Incredibly, in the eight months since Bunker Hill, neither Gage nor Howe, who succeeded to the command in October, had seized Dorchester Heights. On the night of March 4, the patriots

TWENTY FOUR SHILLINGS

Issued in defence of American Liberty

Ense petit placidam sub Libertate Quietem

Augt 18. 1775.

The paper money above, designed by the ever-useful Paul Revere for the commonwealth of Massachusetts, was issued in bold defiance of English law even before independence was declared. The notes were handsome, but soon depreciated, and some of them wound up as wallpaper in barbershops.

did so under cover of a bombardment, and fortified the hill at a feverish pace. When Howe looked up at the heights the next morning he was reported to have said that "the rebels" had done more work in one night than his whole army could have done in six months. Unfavorable weather gave Howe an excuse for not mounting a counterattack, and he decided that his only course was to pull out of Boston. On March 17, 1776 (still celebrated in Boston as Evacuation Day), Howe and his army sailed for Halifax, Nova Scotia, accompanied by crowds of weeping Tories.

Despite enormous provocation, the patriots had refrained from declaring their independence from England, but that had not deterred them from mounting an offensive outside the territory of the Thirteen Colonies. Congress, in September 1775, heartened by the successes around Ticonderoga, authorized an invasion of Canada. This was to anticipate and frustrate the attack on New York which Sir Guy Carleton, British commander in Canada, was planning; and it could possibly make Canada the 14th colony, despite an alien tongue and a different religion. The patriot expedition was led by Brigadier General Richard Montgomery, a British-trained officer, who was aggressive and levelheaded. But the campaign dragged. The fort at St. Johns was retaken from the British after a two-month siege. On November 13, 1775, Montreal fell, and Carleton barely managed to escape to Quebec, the patriots' next objective.

Montgomery drove northeastward from Montreal, and Benedict Arnold moved northwestward from Maine. Arnold's 650 men hacked through the nearly unpenetrable Maine wilderness to join Montgomery's 300 troops. Then everything went wrong. At dawn on December 31, an assault on Quebec's citadel during a raging blizzard ended disastrously for the Americans. Montgomery was dead, Arnold wounded, and nearly 100 other casualties and over 300 prisoners were left behind on the Plains of Abraham. This victory encouraged Carleton to mount his own offensive against New York. The key to successful invasion was the control of Lake Champlain. An alert Sir Guy and a recovered Arnold set to work with all speed to assemble and build ships on the lake for their respective fleets. On October 11, 1776, the powerfully gunned British ships crippled most of the American flotilla at Valcour Bay. Although Arnold's remaining ships, their oars muffled, slipped by the British that night, his flotilla was destroyed as a fighting force two days later. But Arnold's gallant stand had upset Carleton's invasion schedule. Winter had set in; it was no time for fighting. The appraisal of Valcour Bay by Admiral Alfred T. Mahan, the American naval historian, is worth remembering: "Never had any force, big or small, lived to better purpose, or died more gloriously. That the Americans were strong enough to impose the capitulation of Saratoga was due to the invaluable year of delay secured to them by their little navy on Lake Champlain."

PERHAPS the biggest single mistake the British made in the entire Revolutionary War was their decision to abandon their efforts in New England and to probe for spots in the colonies where the rebel spark was reputedly weakest: New York, or Philadelphia, or the South. Experience should have taught them that Virginia was as vigorously insurgent as New England. When Governor Dunmore had tried to whip the Virginia militia in December 1775, his men were mowed down by the rebels at Great Bridge. The survivors had

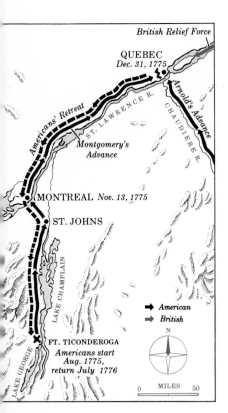

FIRST MAJOR DEFEAT:

QUEBEC, 1775-1776

The first American offensive was a two-pronged attack on Quebec. One prong, led by Benedict Arnold, marched from Boston across Maine. The second, commanded by Richard Montgomery following Philip Schuyler's illness, went on along the St. Lawrence from Ticonderoga, taking St. Johns and Montreal on the way. They lost Ethan Allen, who was captured by the British at Montreal. Montgomery also lost numbers of troops whose enlistments had run out. But he pressed onward to Quebec, where he was killed and both his and Arnold's forces were defeated.

to withdraw to their ships in Norfolk harbor, leaving that town to the rebels.

Learning little from this action, North Carolina's royal governor Josiah Martin then encouraged a group of Loyalists, mostly Scottish, to try to fight their way to the coast and the safety of the British warships. On February 27, 1776, at Moore's Creek Bridge, the rebels stopped this trek, capturing 850 Highlanders in plaids and kilts. Thus royal government ended ignominiously in the plantations of Virginia and North Carolina. Nonetheless, the British were still convinced that the lower South was loyal to George III, a conviction that prompted yet another great strategic blunder. Instead of concentrating their forces for one overpowering blow which would destroy the main Continental army, the British divided their troops.

In June of '76, Commodore Sir Peter Parker and General Henry Clinton mounted a languidly paced amphibious operation against Charleston. But the South Carolinians were well prepared and in a fighting mood, and their main defenses, ingeniously constructed of palmetto logs, soaked up salvos of naval cannon balls like a sponge. The rebels under Colonel William Moultrie gave better than they received; their shore batteries ripped the British ships, littering their decks with "blood and entrails," and inflicted on the commodore himself a slight but humiliating wound which left "his backside laid bare." Clinton abandoned his halfhearted military effort, to his own "unspeakable mortification," and the battered British turned toward New York.

Frustrated in the South, the British now took aim at the Middle States, intending to seize the Hudson and cut the colonies in two. Sailing from Halifax, General Howe was to transport his strengthened forces to New York and later push north along the Hudson to link with Carleton's army coming down from Canada. Benedict Arnold delayed Carleton at Valcour Bay, but Howe's part began exactly as planned. The attack upon New York City involved by far the biggest fighting force America had ever seen: some 32,000 disciplined, professional soldiers (about 9,000 of them German mercenaries) and over 350 ships manned by 10,000 sailors. General Howe commanded the army; his brother Richard, Admiral Lord Howe, the navy. But the brothers Howe came with a laurel wreath as well as a sword. They were named not only to subdue the rebellious colonists but also to act as peace commissioners under authority of Parliament. They bungled their initial attempt at conciliation, however, sending their first letter to "George Washington, Esq." instead of "General George Washington"; Washington stiffly refused it.

In expectation of the British attack, Washington had begun moving troops to New York as early as March. His army was badly outmanned, yet the city could not be abandoned without putting up a fight. Washington fortified Brooklyn Heights and placed half his army there—an almost fatal mistake. And Howe had learned the lesson of Bunker Hill. This time, the British landed in the American rear, cut off the fortified area by flanking actions and thus trapped its defenders. Again displaying his cautious streak, Howe lost a fine chance to end the war by capturing the American army. He waited two days— two days too long. For Washington, appreciating at last the grave peril of his position, effected a masterly withdrawal on the foggy night of August 29-30 before the British could use their fleet to bar a river crossing. Colonel John Glover's skillful fishermen-soldiers from Marblehead and Salem safely ferried 9,500 American soldiers, with all their baggage, guns and horses, over to Man-

FIRST MAJOR VICTORY: BOSTON, 1775-1776

Following Lexington and Concord, siege was laid to Boston. Famous British generals arriving on the scene were not amused by British wits who jeered: "Burgoyne, Clinton and Howe; Bow, Wow, Wow." On June 16, 1775, the Americans occupied Bunker Hill, threatening Boston from the north. Howe and Clinton swept them off, but at a fearful cost in lives. On July 2 Washington took command. On March 4, 1776, ready at last, he fortified Dorchester Heights, his cannon threatening enemy ships. On March 17 the British, deciding to fight somewhere else, departed.

13

hattan. Though suffering the heavier casualties, the bulk of the American army had been saved to fight again.

After the British victory on Long Island, the Howe brothers tried once again to start peace talks. Three members of the rebel Congress, Benjamin Franklin, John Adams, and Edward Rutledge of South Carolina, finally did meet with Lord Howe on Staten Island. But it was too late. While the Howes could pardon and make recommendations, they were not empowered to deal with either an independent Congress or independent states, and the proclamation of independence on July 4 had outdated even the proposals for reconciliation made by the most liberal British faction.

Now even lethargic Sir Billy Howe could not be denied New York. September was a month of indecision for the Americans. "We cannot stay and yet we do not know how to go—so that we may be properly said to be between hawk and buzzard," confessed Washington's adjutant general, Joseph Reed. At length Washington decided New York City was untenable and planned to withdraw to Westchester. The British, meanwhile, had prepared an encircling action to trap the rebel army on Manhattan Island. Covered by shelling from five warships, Clinton's troops landed at Kip's Bay on the morning of September 15. The American militia fled.

There is a time-hallowed—and romanticized—story that British pursuit halted at Murray Hill for nearly two hours while General Howe sipped wine at

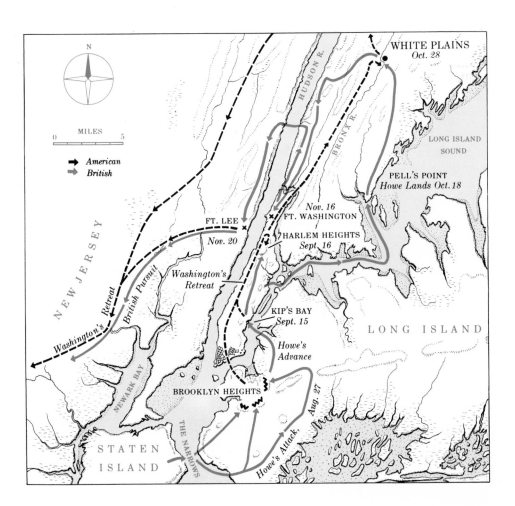

BATTLES FOR NEW YORK
AUG.-NOV. 1776

On Long Island, General Washington's flank was crushed and he was trapped, his back against the East River. But Howe paused and the Americans escaped. When the British landed at Kip's Bay, patriot troops were caught in lower Manhattan; the British waited for reinforcements and the Americans got away. Through the fall of 1776, Washington and Howe matched blunders. When it was all over, Howe had New York, and a comfortable winter's billet. But Washington, because his army had been saved from total destruction, was on his way to winning the war.

the residence of Mrs. Robert Murray. In the interval, Israel Putnam abandoned his supplies and most of his cannon, but got his men back to the American line at Harlem Heights. According to a regimental commander, Colonel George Weedon, Washington was so exasperated at the failure of his troops to make the slightest stand at Kip's Bay that "he struck several officers in their flight, three times dashed his hatt on the ground, and at last exclaimed, 'Good God! Have I got such troops as those?'" Washington himself had to be led off the field to prevent his being captured by the British.

Howe's failure to follow up the Kip's Bay rout gave Washington a chance to strengthen his defenses at Harlem Heights. When British reconnaissance troops incautiously approached the American camp just north of Manhattanville, Washington sent flankers to get into their rear, and began a frontal attack as well. At Harlem Heights the British were forced to yield ground for the first time in the New York campaign.

On September 20 a great fire consumed an extensive area between Broadway and the Hudson River—almost half the city. Howe's taste of victory now turned to ashes. The British blamed the rebels, but a shift of wind and disorganized fire companies were largely responsible. Indeed, Washington's staff had advised him to destroy the town to prevent it from serving as winter headquarters for the British, but he did not feel that his instructions from Congress justified so drastic an action.

Leaving a strong holding force in Fort Washington at the northern tip of Manhattan Island, Washington moved his main army to Westchester. In an effort to outflank the Americans, Howe landed an advance force at Throg's Neck. When his men were thrown back in confusion by a small detachment of Pennsylvania riflemen, he made another landing, this time three miles east at Pell's Point. But the main American army had withdrawn to White Plains to escape encirclement, leaving Colonel John Glover to fight a valiant delaying action against the British near Pelham. Finally, after obtaining Hessian reinforcements, Howe confronted Washington at White Plains on October 28. The British general forced the Americans to fall back, but let victory slip from his grasp when he delayed his attack to await reinforcements. Then, while Howe was held up by a storm, Washington was able to pull back his forces to North Castle, preserving intact the main American army. In this series of moves it is likely that Howe had once again lost his chance to end the war.

Then, on November 16, disaster struck the patriot army. Ignoring the main American force, Howe turned south against Fort Washington on Manhattan Island. Nathanael Greene, who was in command of this strong point, made a costly blunder when he decided against evacuation. Though the British suffered heavily, they captured the fort together with 2,800 prisoners, one of the greatest hauls of the whole war.

AND SO, as the year 1776 drew to a close, the main American army, fewer than 6,000 men, had fled from the New York area and was in full retreat across New Jersey, leaving the British in undisputed possession of the most strategically located harbor on the Atlantic coast. With winter coming on, a British observer remarked that "many of the Rebels who were killed . . . were without shoes or Stockings, & Several were observed to have only linen drawers . . . without any proper shirt or Waistcoat. . . . They must suffer extremely." They did. But the pamphleteering philosopher Tom Paine, who was with

Yankee ingenuity erupted in this hand-propelled submarine—the first ever to see action in battle. Invented by a handy-andy named David Bushnell, the tiny "Turtle" tried to sink H.M.S. "Eagle" off Governors Island in 1776. The attempt turned out to be a noisy failure, but the startled British fled.

them, reported that the soldiers bore their suffering "with a manly and martial spirit." Paine also wrote some moving words which can stand as the slogan of the battered, limping, yet always dangerous little Continental Army: "Tyranny, like hell, is not easily conquered; yet we have this consolation with us, that the harder the conflict, the more glorious the triumph."

The patriots had no illusions about the desperate tasks ahead. Against them were arrayed the vast maritime and financial resources that a powerful world empire could marshal, and a monarch whose stubborn determination to suppress the revolt verged on fanaticism. The victories around New York had shown the ease with which the Royal Navy could support the transport and landing of troops while guarding supply lines at sea. In addition to the mercenaries hired by its ample treasury, Britain enjoyed overwhelming superiority in the number of ground troops. Royal forces also had the prospect of Trojan horse assistance from American Tories—but this never developed in sufficient strength to make an important difference in the fighting.

Considering the odds against them, what kept sensible patriots from realizing that their cause was hopeless? Why was there no serious attempt to make the best possible terms with the king? To be sure, the rebels counted on some very tangible assets. They held the ground and had to be displaced. They were campaigning in familiar country. Their men were accustomed to the use of firearms. And they did possess, although in limited quantities, the Pennsylvania rifle that boasted three times the range of the British smoothbore musket and had far greater accuracy. (Although widely but wrongly called the Kentucky rifle, the long rifle was the product of skilled Pennsylvania gunsmiths.) But their army, as Henry Knox noted, was still untrained, badly officered and "a receptacle for ragamuffins." It was plagued by short-term enlistments and by critical shortages of ammunition, food, clothing and medical supplies. However, it was an army of the people, fighting for a cause that to many meant more than life itself.

There were solid advantages, but they were heavily undercut by the patriots' lack of an effective naval arm to slice the supply line between England

Charles Willson Peale, the American artist-soldier, sketched this Revolutionary War cannon. One of 13 kinds the patriots used, it was probably captured from the British. Peale, an army captain who fought at Trenton, was fascinated by weaponry and often took time out from battles to make drawings. "He fit and painted," remembered a suborainate, "painted and fit."

and Halifax or to prevent the Royal Navy's powerful squadrons from blockading American ports at will. Worse still, the patriots lacked a government with the power to act effectively in wartime, to levy taxes, provide funds and supplies for the army, and prevent the twin threats of inflation and bankruptcy from hamstringing the war effort.

That America won its independence despite a military balance sheet loaded so heavily in Britain's favor seemed miraculous to contemporaries, as it still does. True, the American cause was sustained by the aid received from the French under the alliance made in 1778, but it is fair to say that the British were fatally weakened not only by the adverse factor of geography but also because of errors of strategy and consistent miscalculation of their adversary's powers of resistance. The long, thin line of supply that had to be maintained placed a constant strain upon England's naval effort. This difficulty was compounded by the defects of leadership, both civilian and military.

The British leaders were cocky and overconfident at the start. They made the fatal mistake of underestimating their opponents and of entrusting the immediate direction of the war to mediocrities and worse. It is incomprehensible, for example, that Lord George Germain, who had been court-martialed for cowardice in 1760, found guilty and declared "unfit to serve his Majesty in any military capacity whatsoever," should still be Secretary of State for the Colonies, responsible for the conduct of the army in the field. The profligate and corrupt Earl of Sandwich, First Lord of the Admiralty, was hampered in his feeble efforts to build a fighting navy by the penny-pinching policies of Lord North and the king, but Sandwich himself also failed to use the navy to establish a tight blockade of the American coast. George III, who consistently indulged in wishful thinking, regularly intruded his advice on military and naval matters, and his prejudices could not be lightly disregarded.

When William Pitt heard the names of the officers appointed to command in the war against America, he is said to have exclaimed: "I do not know what effect these names have on the enemy, but I confess they make *me* tremble." Commanders like Gage, Howe and Clinton lacked both high ability and readiness to seize the initiative. And the pair who did take real risks, Burgoyne and Cornwallis, suffered total defeat. Before long, most Englishmen were ready to throw up their hands in despair.

I F the British lost their first empire because of repeated blunders of immense magnitude, the patriots achieved independence because they retained the will to continue fighting—this despite raw troops, enemies within and without, greed and self-interest, parochial and sectional rivalries, and the passive resistance of men of little faith.

The colonists' will to win was superbly exemplified by their commanding officer. In George Washington the patriots had found a leader whom they soon recognized as the indispensable symbol of selfless patriotism and integrity, a man possessed of both the intellect and the resiliency to rebound after faltering mistakes and reverses. Capable of delivering lightning blows of his own, Washington was prepared to share with his army the ordeals of Valley Forge and Morristown, ready to stand up against the men in Congress and in the army who placed selfish interests above country. Most important of all, he was able by sheer domination of will and single-minded dedication to keep his army an effective fighting force until victory.

Elaborately dressed in spotless linens and tassels, the military dandy above is a picture drawn by a Hessian officer of his American adversary, right down to the musket and bayonet. But in truth, patriot soldiers often looked like civilians. They wore homespuns and buckskins adorned with different colored cockades and ribbands to distinguish their ranks.

Embattled farmer-militia dig in near Bunker Hill the night before the British attack of June 17, 1775.

First blows in the war for freedom

THE Revolutionary War began with a great toppling of royal emblems and a rush of citizens to arms around Boston. Opposed to the rebels were British General Gage's 4,000 men, the main British force in the colonies. As the fighting went on, Britain brought over as many as 55,000 soldiers, including about 30,000 German-speaking mercenaries; to these were added many American Tories and Indians. The redcoats generally were well equipped; although their heavy muskets were dismally inaccurate, they were supplemented by that very useful weapon, the glittering, 21-inch bayonet.

The American troops were drawn from a colonial population of more than two million, of which some 500,000 were Tory sympathizers. Although there were over 200,000 enlistments during the war, Washington in fact never had more than 8,000 Continental regulars in a single battle. The short-term militia sometimes performed magnificently (at Bunker Hill and Bennington) and sometimes ran away (at Kip's Bay and White Plains). But by living to fight another day, they effectively foiled the British strategy, which was to split the colonies in two and destroy American fighting power in a series of quick, smashing blows.

JUBILANT PATRIOTS pull down the mounted figure of George III in New York City on July 9, 1776. On the same day, the Declaration of Independence was read publicly in New York for the first time. The 4,000 pounds of lead in the statue was converted into musket balls so that, as one New Yorker cheerfully wrote, the king's men could feel the effect of "melted Majesty fired at them."

At Lexington, outnumbered minutemen are shot down by the British. But one unawed colonial (lower left) shakes his fist at the redcoats.

Bloodstains on a peaceful village green

THE picture above is as close as one can get to an eye-witness view of the action at Lexington, Massachusetts, early in the morning of April 19, 1775. Some days later Ralph Earl, a Connecticut artist, made sketches on the spot (and at Concord) which were engraved by his friend Amos Doolittle. From this historic record it is obvious that the minutemen at Lexington had not picked a fight with the much larger British force: most of them had turned to retreat before the heavy firing began. Old Jonas Parker, who ignored his captain's command to retreat, was knocked down by a British ball and run through with a bayonet while on the ground. Young Jonathan Harrington, whose wife and small son were watching, crawled 100 yards across the grass to die on his own doorstep. One British private was slightly wounded. Eight Americans were dead, 10 wounded.

This should have taught the Yankees a lesson. Instead, militia from half a dozen towns gathered near the North Bridge in Concord while the redcoats searched the town for military supplies. Returning British fire, the Americans cleared the bridge, as shown in the sketch at far right, and then moved off. Later they joined the steadily arriving militiamen who were lining the road to Boston. When the much too leisurely British finally started back to their base, the day's real slaughter began: minutemen swarming behind the stone fences inflicted 273 casualties—73 dead, 174 wounded, 26 missing—in revenge for the patriots' losses at Lexington.

At Concord, British officers (right) reconnoiter as troops search the town. Forewarned, the colonists had moved much of their vital supplies.

FIRST ATTACK by Americans against a body of organized British troops is launched at old North Bridge near Concord. The minutemen, seeing smoke, suspected the British of burning homes and acted to stop them. Only a few on each side were killed in this fight, but these were the shots "... heard round the world."

BOSTON

BUNKER HILL, unseen beyond the crest of Breed's Hill *(top right)*, is the final objective of the redcoats lined up for their brave uphill assault. But so costly was the victory on these two hills that the British knew their Boston troops alone could never win the war. In this early American painting, Charlestown village is burning briskly under the British bombardment.

CHARLES TOWN

THE STARTLED COMMANDER of the British garrison at Ticonderoga *(opposite)* stares at sword-waving Ethan Allen. So swift were the patriots that the British officer next to Allen was captured before he had time to put on a pair of pants.

A GENIAL GUNNER, Henry Knox's military bearing *(right)* started high because of the paunch below. An energetic officer, he did a fine job of guiding the "noble train of artillery" captured at Ticonderoga over almost impassable roads to Boston.

The guns of Ticonderoga and the liberation of Boston

ETHAN ALLEN, a hotheaded Vermont farmer, scored the colonies' first victory. Commanding the Green Mountain Boys, a force originally raised to drive out New Yorkers claiming possession of Vermont, he and Benedict Arnold captured a fortful of guns *(opposite)* at Ticonderoga on Lake Champlain in May 1775. Later Allen's burning devotion to his state would lead him to offer the British a separate peace provided they would recognize Vermont as an entity, independent of its hated enemies, New York and New Hampshire. But in 1775 he was everybody's hero. Up to the fort came austere Philip Schuyler to plot the invasion of Canada. And from Massachusetts came Henry Knox, the ever-optimistic Boston bookseller, to claim the guns for General Washington.

Knox's winter trek hauled the guns to Dorchester Heights above Boston early in 1776, forcing the British to evacuate the town in March.

LOFTY CITADEL of Quebec towers above the St. Lawrence. This view, drawn around 1777 by an English engineer who charted the area, shows the fort as invading Americans saw it.

A bold assault defeated inside the walls of Quebec

OLD Samuel de Champlain's fortress city of Quebec frowned on generals. Wolfe died assaulting it, Montcalm died defending it. Now came the turn of Richard Montgomery of Dublin, Ireland, late captain in His Majesty's 17th Foot and present brigadier general in the Continental army. Montgomery had learned his soldiering fighting the French and Indians along Lake Champlain, then took postgraduate courses at the sieges of Havana and Martinique. Later he farmed a little near New York City, then farmed much more after he married Janet, daughter of wealthy Robert R. Livingston, and settled at Grassmere, her estate near Rhinebeck. By wish and by wedlock American, Montgomery was named second to Major General Philip Schuyler, commanding the invasion of Canada. When Schuyler fell ill Montgomery took charge. At St. Johns he captured the colors of the 7th Fusiliers—first British flags to fall to the Americans. He moved on to take Montreal and join Benedict Arnold's weary troops at Quebec. Behind the town's walls the British had been busy preparing a snare for their old friend and fellow officer. The maze of winding lanes, cunningly spotted with snipers' posts, turned and twisted in all directions and ended in cul-de-sacs. On the last day of 1775, Montgomery's assaulting force was caught in these alleys and there, leading his bewildered troops, the general was shot dead.

The wintry death of heroic Montgomery is depicted in a Trumbull

26

painting. *Captain Jacob Cheeseman, at the general's knees, had put five gold pieces in his pocket to pay for burying "him with decency."*

An old mill beside Gowanus Creek is the center of hard fighting during the battle of Long Island. Here Maryland and Delaware troops

A strategic British victory and a providential fire

During the summer of 1776 an awesome array of British might converged on the lower Hudson River. There were plenty of men, tons of supplies and an overwhelming armada of ships—all that seemed necessary to end the war in a hurry. The bloodletting around Boston and the American fiasco in Canada had been, in a sense, preliminary bouts. Now the main event could begin.

The British had evacuated Boston on March 17. Washington guessed that their next destination would be New York. "It is the Place that we must use every Endeavour to keep from them," he wrote. "For should they get that Town . . . they can stop the Intercourse between the northern and southern Colonies, upon which depends the Safety of America." But how could the island town of New York be defended against British sea power?

Washington was still an inexperienced general. He divided his army between Manhattan and Brooklyn. But guided by Tory farmers from Flatbush, Howe's army surrounded the advance American posts on the morning of August 27. What followed was the war's first pitched battle between armies *(above),* a confused melee in which the Americans were driven back by irresistible numbers and barely escaped to their boats, losing more than a thousand casualties and prisoners.

On September 15, protected by bombardment from British warships stationed in the East River, 9,000 redcoats and Hessians made a successful landing at rocky Kip's Bay on the island of Manhattan. The American militia who were there to oppose them were so terrified by the ships' cannon that they threw down their guns and ran. Washington encountered them in full flight. "Take the walls! Take the cornfield!" he cried, and tried to flog them into line with his riding cane. His only consolation came when an unexplained fire destroyed much of the city on September 20, depriving the British of winter housing. "Providence," wrote the grim American commander, "or some good honest fellow, has done more for us than we were disposed to do for ourselves."

retreat across the creek after staving off the British attack long enough to help save the main American army in Brooklyn Heights.

TRIUMPHAL ENTRY of British into New York, as imagined by Herr Habermann of Augsburg, is seen in a 1776 print for peep show exhibits. Such "re-creations" were popular in Germany.

GREAT FIRE which followed the British victory is another one of Herr Habermann's many fabrications. Any pictures of revolutionary America found appreciative audiences in Europe.

A disaster and an escape

STILL hoping to hold the Hudson, Washington concentrated men and artillery in Fort Washington and Fort Lee, on opposite sides of the river, north of New York City. But British ships sailed past the American guns at will. Knowledge of British plans was sparse; a major spy mission failed when Nathan Hale *(below)* was seized before he could transmit military secrets. By November, Washington had almost decided to evacuate Fort Washington. Before a decision was reached, British troops, under cover of cannon fire, ferried the Harlem and overwhelmed the defenders. The surrender of Fort Washington was a stupendous American loss.

To complete the disaster, the British scaled the New Jersey Palisades *(right)* and moved quickly against Fort Lee. The garrison fled and joined Washington's main army in its retreat across New Jersey. But they had lost all their blankets and tents, and winter was setting in. Yet there was no capitulation. Instead, the hard-pressed Continentals braced themselves for the conflict ahead.

AN AMERICAN SPY, Nathan Hale gives his life for his country on September 22, 1776. Fully aware of the risk, he had volunteered for a mission behind enemy lines.

BRITISH ATTACKERS swarm up the Palisades to seize Fort Lee, New Jersey. This watercolor was made by a British officer, Thomas Davies, who was an eyewitness.

2. THE GREAT DECLARATION

THE American Revolution was an event of enormous complexity and magnitude. Starting as a series of skirmishes for the defense of colonial rights, it exploded into a full-scale war for political independence, and unleashed pent-up demands for political and social reform. It was also a civil war which, if it did not pit section against section or class against class, divided American families, neighbors and villages. Englishmen, too, took sides, though their battles were confined to Parliament and the press.

The Revolution has been called a war fought both for home rule and to decide who should rule at home. But it was more than that. It was a very important part of a world war, primarily between England and France, that was fought at Gibraltar, along the coast of India and off South Africa, as well as on Lake Champlain, the Chesapeake and the Caribbean. And a large part of Europe was drawn into the conflict.

Unlike most revolutions that followed, this one was distinguished by a deep concern for, and emphatic stress upon, legality. The Americans fought for the rights they believed were guaranteed them as Englishmen under the British constitution, and for the rights of man as they understood them to be derived from the "Laws of Nature and of Nature's God."

The war was not entered into precipitously; its leadership throughout remained in the hands of prudent, civilized men whose respect for legality is best seen in the reluctance with which they severed their formal ties to Britain.

SYMBOLS OF INDEPENDENCE, recalling the battles which led up to the Declaration, surround the portraits of distinguished signer John Adams and his beloved wife Abigail.

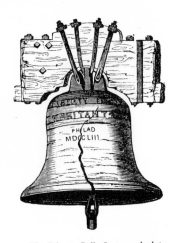

The Liberty Bell, first cracked in testing on its arrival from England in 1752, was not recast and hung until 1753. Long after ringing independence, it was cracked once more and finally silenced on Washington's birthday in 1846. It was called the "Liberty Bell" in antislavery propaganda in 1839.

A TORY JIBE OF 1776

*These hardy knaves and stupid
   fools,
Some apish and pragmatic mules,
Some servile acquiescing tools,—
These, these compose the Congress!*

*When Jove resolved to send a curse,
And all the woes of life rehearse,
Not plague, not famine, but much
   worse—
He cursed us with a Congress.*

In 1774 the First Continental Congress had asserted the rights of America, denounced the "wicked ministry" of the British government and embarked on a boycott of British goods. Parliament's response on February 9, 1775, to Congress' petition for a redress of grievances was to declare Massachusetts in a state of rebellion. The Second Congress, which convened in 1775, organized an army and a navy—and even sought foreign aid. Still it refrained from disowning the sovereign. As late as July 1775, weeks after the bloody Battle of Bunker Hill, Congress adopted the so-called "Olive Branch Petition," which John Dickinson of Pennsylvania drafted. It expressed hope for harmony and pleaded with the king to halt further hostile steps against the colonies until a reconciliation could be worked out. True, John Adams, representative of the more extreme New England faction, tartly observed that "Mr. Dickinson gives a silly cast to our doings," but Dickinson much more than Adams voiced the go-slow mood of Congress in the summer of '75.

That mood may have been conservative; it was scarcely submissive. Two days earlier, Congress had adopted another resolution which, while rejecting independence, asserted America's readiness to die rather than be enslaved.

The "Olive Branch Petition" was hailed by the Earl of Shelburne, a close student of American affairs, as "the fairest foundation for an honourable and advantageous accommodation." But with characteristic stubbornness, George III refused even to receive it and on August 23, 1775, he proclaimed the colonists in a state of rebellion and threatened with "condign punishment the authors, perpetrators, and abetters of such traitorous designs."

For almost 15 months, colonists fought redcoats without a formal declaration of war or a formal proclamation of independence. But the people were not as patient or cautious as their leaders. The tide of independence had surged on, coming to full flood by the late spring of '76. Throughout the Thirteen Colonies, there was a recognition of common interests and a growing sense of separateness—even in speech—from the mother country. (As early as 1756, Dr. Samuel Johnson noted the "American dialect.") More significantly, Americans no longer thought of themselves as Europeans.

One further element, a budding psychological unity among the colonists, helped create an "American nationalism." Patrick Henry in 1774 had electrified the First Continental Congress in Philadelphia when he declared, "The distinctions between Virginians, Pennsylvanians, New Yorkers, and New Englanders are no more. I am not a Virginian, but an American." And America, the colonists felt, was a purer land than Europe, a refuge for the poor and the oppressed, a spot where "fair freedom shall forever reign," as Philip Freneau phrased it in 1771. A decade later, Hector St. John Crèvecoeur, a Frenchman residing in America, was to write, in his *Letters from an American Farmer*, of this land where "individuals of all nations are melted into a new race of men," and of the "western pilgrims" who would one future day bring about great change in the world.

Despite the growth of nationalism by 1775, few Americans of prominence attributed their wrongs to George III himself. Most Americans considered the crown above criticism. But there were exceptions. Some Anglican churchmen suspected religious dissenters of antimonarchism, and there were New England preachers like Jonathan Mayhew who were outspoken in their republicanism. As early as 1763, Patrick Henry had denounced the king as a tyrant, but he was haranguing a jury, not making a responsible public utterance. Sam

Adams and his friends who harbored similar views represented a minority.

Since it is human nature to personalize grievances, George III, who took so direct a part in his ministry's decisions, could not long escape attack by his American subjects. In January 1776, Tom Paine, the son of a Quaker corset-maker and himself only recently arrived in America, issued a ringing call to independence in his memorable pamphlet "Common Sense," which assailed both monarchy as an institution and the monarch as a person. Paine demolished the distinction between the king (the "Royal Brute," he called him) and his ministry on the one hand, and between the king and his Parliament on the other. Paine's pamphlet had an enormous readership and greatly increased the sentiment for independence.

Aᴸᴸ along, the king and his government had failed to understand the temper of the Americans, treating the colonists like rebellious children instead of mature, literate and capable citizens. Now the cabinet took a step that aroused the deepest aversion: they decided to use foreign mercenaries as a punitive force. They justified their decision by confessing that, since there was little or no enthusiasm among Englishmen to enlist for the war in America, they had to rent troops from the Continent to bolster the regulars. Besides, Lord North admitted, it was cheaper. After being turned down by Catherine the Great of Russia, who thought the king's handling of the colonies was pretty stupid, the ministry hired soldiers from six petty German rulers. In Edmund Burke's wonderful phrase, these six "snuffed the cadaverous taint of lucrative war." Of the 30,000 German troops brought to America, more than half were furnished by the Landgrave of Hesse-Cassel, so the word "Hessian" came to be loosely applied to all the German mercenaries. The use of Hessians was overwhelmingly endorsed in Parliament despite the opposition in Commons by pro-Americans like Burke and Charles James Fox, and by the latter's uncle, the Duke of Richmond, in the Lords. All of the early war measures taken by Lord North's ministry were similarly approved.

If British intransigence and the dispatch of foreign troops sparked the nationalist sentiment in America, timely patriot propaganda constantly fed the flames. Paine's eloquent pen clothed the colonists' struggle with nobility. He reminded his readers that "the sun never shined on a cause of greater worth," that "now is the seedtime of continental union, faith and honor," and that America embodied the cause of freedom. "O ye that love mankind!" Paine exhorted. "Ye that dare oppose not only the tyranny but the tyrant, stand forth! . . . Freedom hath been hunted round the globe. . . . O receive the fugitive, and prepare in time an asylum for mankind."

In May of '76, John Adams could write that "every post and every day rolls in upon us Independence like a torrent." By that date the more radical patriots, save in the Middle States, had won control of their respective governments and committed them to independence. By implication South Carolina's new constitution repudiated the Loyalists. Other states instructed their delegates to support independence, and during May and June one town meeting after another in Massachusetts approved it. On May 15, Edmund Pendleton, a moderate, pushed through the Virginia Convention a unanimous resolution for independence. The time for a complete break with England had come. On June 7, Richard Henry Lee of Virginia put before the Continental Congress the momentous resolution calling for a declaration of independence, foreign

A stylish orator, Richard Henry Lee of Virginia was once accused of rehearsing his gestures before a mirror. He was an early critic of British policies, and helped found intercolony Committees of Correspondence. After presenting a resolution for independence, he battled hard for the Bill of Rights.

THE SIGNERS

CONNECTICUT

Sam¹ Huntington

Roger Sherman

Wᵐ Williams

Oliver Wolcott

DELAWARE

Tho M:Kean

Geo Read

Caesar Rodney

GEORGIA

Button Gwinnett

Lyman Hall

Geo Walton

MARYLAND

Charles Carroll of Carrollton

Samuel Chase

Wᵐ Paca

Thoˢ Stone

alliances and a confederation of the American states. After a stirring debate on July 1, there was an indecisive vote. South Carolina and Pennsylvania were against independence. Delaware's delegation was divided, while New York's representatives awaited instructions from their state. An impasse seemed likely, but the radicals worked feverishly to override the opposition. Caesar Rodney arrived in time to swing Delaware's vote to independence; South Carolina switched sides; two Pennsylvanians did not attend and one changed his mind, swaying that colony to independence. Through these maneuvers, the Congress was able to vote unanimously for independence on July 2. The "patricians" might "stamp and foam and curse, but all in vain," John Adams wrote triumphantly. "The decree is gone forth."

ALL that remained was for Congress to justify its stand before the world. Back in June it had appointed a committee to spell out the reasons for the anticipated move, naming Thomas Jefferson, Benjamin Franklin, John Adams, Robert R. Livingston and Roger Sherman. The committee designated Jefferson to prepare a draft. The 33-year-old Virginian had already won recognition by his eloquent and persuasive arguments in several state papers, and Franklin and Adams made only minor changes in Jefferson's version of the Declaration. Further emendations and revisions came during the debates in Congress. Notably, a clause criticizing the English people was struck out, as was another indicting George III for forcing African slaves on the colonies. The former was omitted to avoid offending some of America's strong friends in England; the latter, in deference to the lower South, although, as Jefferson caustically remarked, "Our Northern brethren . . . felt a little tender under those censures; for tho' their people have very few slaves themselves, yet they had been pretty considerable carriers of them to others."

The Declaration was a persuasive, eloquent and unforgettable statement of the "causes" which forced the colonies to dissolve their "political bands" and "to assume among the powers of the earth, the separate and equal station to which the laws of nature and of nature's God entitle them." It was a truly explosive combination of skillful propaganda and trenchant political reasoning. It was a ringing assertion of the right to revolt, carefully erected upon the principle that government ultimately rests upon the consent of the governed. It enumerated the significant personal rights that public government must preserve, rights which embraced life, liberty and "the pursuit of happiness," the last a felicitous phrase covering individual liberty, freedom of vocational choice, and full property rights.

Perhaps the way the Declaration raised the sights and objectives of the Revolution was even more important than its enunciation of broad democratic principles of government and of self-determination. The Declaration set a new standard for a free society. Granted the phrase "all men are created equal" did not accurately describe the America of 1776, where about a half million persons—one fifth of the entire population—were held in slavery, and granted that a good many of the signers must have accepted this phrase with silent reservations, the Declaration nevertheless represented a lofty ideal and a long-range goal. As Lincoln later said of the founding fathers, "They meant to set up a standard maxim for a free society, which could be . . . constantly looked to, constantly labored for, and even though never perfectly attained, constantly approximated, and thereby constantly spreading and deepening its influence and augmenting the happiness and value of life to all people of all colors everywhere." Of all our nobly phrased historic documents, the Declaration has become the most cherished expression of the American dream.

It also made at least one other thing clear: the spirit of that day was critical of existing evils, sympathetic to the winds of change and reform. The Revolution gave substance to what Jefferson called "the unquestionable republicanism of the American mind." For the first time in history, a sizable number of former colonies established their own governments—in all, 11 of the 13 states drew up written constitutions. Only Rhode Island and Connecticut were content to use their old self-governing charters. These state constitutions were mostly the work of revolutionary congresses or conventions, but in Massachusetts a special constitutional convention was summoned and its handiwork was submitted to the people in 1780 for adoption or rejection. Here was a clear precedent both for the Constitutional Convention of 1787 and for the principle that a basic charter should be submitted directly to the people for their ratification.

The new constitutions were remarkably conservative in content, despite the revolutionary concept they signalized and the revolutionary method by which they had been adopted. They leaned heavily on the old colonial charters, because Americans were in the main content with the actual workings of the old colonial governments. The principal changes were in the severe limitations placed on the power of the governor, for most patriots resented the authority held by the old royal representatives.

In consequence, the legislatures which emerged from these state constitutions were powerful. Nearly all were two-chambered bodies, reflecting the organization of Britain's two Houses of Parliament. In most states, only the lower house could originate money bills. Frequent elections, generally for one- or two-year terms, ensured that the legislatures would be responsive to public opinion. Voting was limited to male landholders, renters of houses or taxpayers. High property holdings were still required for officials, somewhat lower for voters. These requirements might not seem very democratic today, but the freehold was so widely distributed in the colonies, and opportunities to acquire property were so abundant, that the suffrage does not appear in fact to have been too restrictive.

A number of state constitutions included sections listing specific natural rights. These included guarantees of personal liberty, freedom of speech and religious worship, as well as security against unreasonable search, excessive bail and fines, and cruel and unusual punishments—all foreshadowing the first 10 amendments to the Constitution, generally called the Bill of Rights.

THE experience of erecting state governments was instructive, but the resulting political separatism among the former colonies raised serious problems. For many patriots, independence without union was inconceivable. "For God's sake let there be a full revolution," wrote the radical New Englander Joseph Hawley, "or all has been done in vain. Independence and a well-planned continental government will save us." Parliament and the king may have rejected the notion of a federal partnership with the colonies, but many Americans favored federalism in some form. The early ideas of union set forth by Franklin at Albany in 1754, then thought too advanced, seemed quite attractive to the First Continental Congress in 1774. Both conservatives

MASSACHUSETTS
John Adams
Sam¹ Adams
Elbridge Gerry
John Hancock
Rob¹ Treat Paine

NEW HAMPSHIRE
Josiah Bartlett
Matthew Thornton
W™ Whipple

NEW JERSEY
Abra Clark
John Hart
Fra⁵ Hopkinson
Rich⁴ Stockton
Jn° Witherspoon

and radicals pushed for some form of federalism, although they would continue to differ on ends and on means. Joseph Galloway, soon to join the Tories, proposed a watered-down version of Franklin's Albany Plan of Union, with one exception: *both* Parliament and the proposed intercolonial council would be empowered to legislate for the colonies, each to have a veto over the other. Indicative of the sentiment for federation, this proposal was defeated by only six states to five.

IN July 1775, at the Second Continental Congress, Franklin proposed a confederation based on his old Albany proposal. The scientist-statesman advocated representation in proportion to population. He was not prepared to grant Congress the power to tax individuals, but he did propose the creation of a "common Treasury" to which each colony would contribute proportionately. Yet the large powers Franklin's new plan conferred on Congress in other respects pointed toward a national sovereignty, notably in granting powers in all matters "necessary to the General Welfare."

Shelved temporarily, Franklin's plan was reworked by a committee that submitted it in July of 1776 under the title "Articles of Confederation and Perpetual Union." This proposal stressed state sovereignty and gave Congress only such limited powers as the right of "determining on peace and war," conducting foreign relations and arbitrating disputes between states. But Congress had neither the power to tax nor to regulate foreign and interstate commerce. It could meet expenses "for the common defense or general welfare" by making requisitions on the states, but taxes could be laid and levied only by the respective legislatures. There were other serious defects: regardless of size or population, each state had just one vote in Congress; no delegate could serve more than three years over a six-year period; all important measures required the assent of nine states; amendments needed the unanimous consent of the state legislatures.

It took Congress nearly 18 months to propose even this frail charter to the states, and they in turn took almost four years to ratify it. Finally, in 1781, the old Congress continued with a new title, "The United States in Congress assembled." Meantime, the administration of the war was divided between Congress and the states, with Congress rather ineffectually combining in itself executive, administrative and legislative functions. To coordinate the war effort of this weak central government and 13 very sovereign states required— as John Adams observed—"the meekness of Moses, the patience of Job and the wisdom of Solomon, added to the valour of David." No such composite Biblical hero emerged. The President of Congress was simply a presiding officer. Without a strong executive or effective taxing powers, Congress had to work through committees and with exhortation. Its committees were racked by personal intrigue, publicity-seeking and sectional rivalries, and lacked first-rate talent. The ablest patriots were sent abroad on foreign assignments, were in the armed services, or (like Virginia's Jefferson and New Jersey's William Livingston) preferred to serve their states as governors. Nonetheless, the congressional committees managed to secure substantial aid from France and Spain, raise funds and supplies both abroad and at home for the army, and give over-all direction to the war effort.

However, by 1781, when the war was fast drawing to a close, Congress had had enough of hydra-headed committees and ventured to experiment with single heads of departments as provided for under the Articles of Confederation. In that year a Superintendent of Finance, a Secretary of Foreign Affairs, a Secretary of War, a Secretary of Marine and a Postmaster were appointed. Thus the first faint foundations were laid for the executive departments whose heads now constitute the United States Cabinet.

The War for Independence clearly worked a great political revolution. Only to a limited extent did it work a social revolution, since it was *not* fought on class lines. Both rich and poor took the patriot side—great landowners like the Van Rensselaers in New York and George Washington in Virginia, great merchants like the Browns of Providence, conservative professional men like John Jay and John Dickinson, along with an array of shopkeepers, farmers, tenants, mechanics, apprentices, hunters, mariners and fishermen. But the Loyalists also recruited large numbers from each of these groups. In one southern area alone, they included 47 merchants, 18 planters, 22 laborers, seven schoolmasters, two keepers of ferries, an organ player and a midwife. For every Edmund Fanning in North Carolina or James Delancey in New York City, there were many Tory small landholders who had fought the patriot landlords in upstate New York or in the back country of the Carolinas. And there were the slaves whose prospects of freedom seemed brighter under the crown than if their owners achieved independence. In fact, no one event in the early part of the war did more to turn uncommitted Southern planters into patriots than the action of the British in seizing and threatening to free the slaves of insurgent planters. By way of contrast, in South Carolina a patriot general, Thomas Sumter, even paid his troops with slaves plundered from the Tories. The pay scale ranged from a colonel's three and a half slaves per year to a private's bounty of one adult slave for each 10-month enlistment.

Such social and economic changes as took place were the consequences rather than the purpose of the war. New events bring up new men and new ideas, but one of the most remarkable aspects of the American Revolution was that its social change was relatively so modest. The estates of conspicuous Tories were indeed confiscated, but this was done to provide a lesson (and a warning) to others and to raise funds desperately needed for the war; there was no intention of redistributing property to the landless. In due course the large confiscated estates often did get into the hands of former tenants and small holders, but initially many parcels were picked up by wealthy patriot speculators. New laws abolished the old European practices of creating large hereditary estates through entailment and primogeniture (the exclusive inheritance of real property by the eldest son). But even in the South, where these practices had been most widespread, the reforms did not prove too consequential, as the wills of most southern planters had for generations made ample provision for younger children.

Some patriots undoubtedly fought the war to rid themselves of debts owed British merchants. In Virginia the debt-burdened tobacco planters (who in 1775 owed London dealers many millions of dollars) rushed a bill through the legislature authorizing the payment into the state loan office of sums due British subjects. After the war, there was resentment and panic when the peace treaty of 1783 seemed to recognize the validity of the prewar debts. "If we are now to pay the debts due the British merchants," George Mason asked Patrick Henry, "what have we been fighting for all this while?" Nevertheless,

RHODE ISLAND

William Ellery

SOUTH CAROLINA

Tho⁵ Heyward Jun!

Thomas Lynch Jun!

Arthur Middleton

Edward Rutledge

VIRGINIA

Carter Braxton

Benj⁴ Harrison

Th Jefferson

Francis Lightfoot Lee

Richard Henry Lee

Tho⁵ Nelson jr.

George Wythe

Independence Hall, once called Pennsylvania State House, was completed around 1756. In 1781 its Liberty Bell was rehung in a clock steeple that replaced the first tower.

39

Gentle George Wythe of Virginia was a distinguished judge and the law professor of Jefferson, John Marshall and Henry Clay. In his will he freed his slaves and left his library to Jefferson. His chief beneficiary, an impatient grandnephew, sped his inheritance by dosing Wythe's coffee with arsenic.

An aristocratic Virginian, Benjamin Harrison was the father of President William Henry Harrison, the great-grandfather of President Benjamin Harrison. He was once called "an indolent, luxurious, heavy gentleman," but he presided effectively over Congress in its vital debate on independence.

the British ultimately collected a substantial part of the debt, and what the planter class gained was precious time.

The era of the American Revolution stimulated broad humanitarian impulses and programs: penal codes were reformed, prison systems reconstituted, and states assumed a greater responsibility for education. A powerful movement for religious toleration, initiated by Jefferson and Madison in Virginia, led to the disestablishment of the Anglican Church in every colony where it had been tax-supported. Even slavery was shaken by the wave of reform. Two northern states abolished slavery, and others adopted systems of gradual emancipation. Many Southerners of this period recognized the evils of slavery and took steps to free their own slaves by deed or will. Patrick Henry reflected the enlightened southern view; he looked forward to the day when "this lamentable evil" would be abolished, though he continued to hold slaves because of "the general inconvenience of living without them." Unhappily, technological change soon fastened the slave system far more firmly into the South's way of life and prevented gradual application of the ideals of equality so nobly phrased by the Revolutionary generation.

The American Revolution, if not a class war, was a vivid example of a civil war. As one Connecticut Tory eloquently and accurately put it, "Nabour was against Nabour, Father against the Son and the son against the Father, and he that would not thrust his one blaid through his brothers heart was cald an Infimous fillon." Consider Benjamin Franklin, most internationally renowned of all the patriots, and his illegitimate son William, the royal governor of New Jersey and a despised Tory leader; Gouverneur Morris and his Tory mother and half brother; James Otis and his Tory wife; John Jay and his neutralist brother Sir James; and many, many other examples of divided families.

John Adams put the Tories (also called Loyalists) at one third of the population; he gave another third to the fence-sitters. While contemporaries and later historians have argued about which side had the numerical preponderance—and the argument still goes on—one fact is clear: a substantial portion of the American people opposed the war and its objectives, and another large, if fluctuating, number switched sides depending on the fortunes of war. The Loyalists came from all classes, but there was a solid representation from employees of the crown and their families and connections, from the prosperous, the propertied, and the clergy of the Church of England. Loyalism was not limited to one section, but it was stronger in the Middle States than in New England, weaker in the upper than in the lower South.

SINCE the Loyalists were considered potential traitors, patriot vigilante committees sought them out and demanded oaths of allegiance to the American cause. Stubborn Tories were subjected to various punishments. These often went so far as tarring and feathering, confiscation of property, banishment and, in a few cases, hanging. To the patriots, the Tories were dangerous. They spied, sold supplies to the British, fought in large numbers in British ranks or in units of their own, did much of the unsavory fighting in the southern uplands and joined with the Indians in the terroristic warfare of the northern borderlands. Tories posed a real and constant peril to the patriot cause, and even men as moderate and judicious as Washington, Franklin and Jay regarded them with loathing and rancor.

As the fortunes of war turned against the Loyalists, they took refuge in such

British-occupied posts as New York, or fled to Halifax. Large numbers of them eventually went into exile in England. Despite the generous treatment meted out to them by the British government, they were unhappy with their lot as expatriates and embittered by the failure of British military efforts. Above all, they were homesick. Perhaps as many as 100,000 Tories, out of the total American population of 2.5 million, left the country, most never to return. The proportionate emigration of the opposition was in fact far higher than in the French Revolution of the following decade, which counted some 120,000 Royalist émigrés in a population of 25 million.

THE French and the American Revolutions had strong connections and resemblances as well as dissimilarities. The French Revolution was brought on by near-bankruptcy, a condition partly attributable to France's expensive efforts to defeat England and—incidentally—secure America's independence. Ideologically, there was a more direct inspiration. The Declaration of the Rights of Man adopted at the start of the French Revolution owed much to the Virginia Bill of Rights and the Declaration of Independence. There were other similarities. Both revolutions stressed legality; both were led at the beginning by a middle-class elite. The leadership of both sprang from the ranks of the ambitious and successful, not from among disgruntled failures. But there was one profound difference. In America, the elite group which began the war managed to remain in control at the end and to make the peace. In France, as Chateaubriand, the author and statesman, wrote, "The patricians began the Revolution, the plebeians finished it."

Another striking difference is that the American Revolution was won without resort either to a bloody reign of terror or to the conservative reaction known as Thermidor. In one respect, at least, the Americans were more ruthless than the French. The Loyalists in the main were banned from returning and their property was permanently confiscated. The Royalist émigrés ultimately came back to France and regained their property. This difference is important. In America today, everybody accepts the Revolution; in France, the extreme Right still opposes the things for which the French Revolution stood, while the extreme Left insists it did not go far enough.

Both events stirred up changes and reforms no one anticipated. Benjamin Rush, the physician-statesman, perceived the dual nature of the American Revolution as early as July 4, 1787, when he said: "There is nothing more common than to confound the terms of the American Revolution with those of the late American War. The American War is over, but this is far from being the case with the American Revolution. On the contrary, nothing but the first act of the great drama is closed."

The succeeding acts of this great turning point of history were to be played on an ever-broadening stage. The implications of the American Revolution would be felt by peoples in nations not yet dreamed of. Bolívar and San Martín, liberators of Spain's colonies in Latin America during the early 19th Century, would be among the many revolutionaries who would take inspiration from America's founding fathers. So were those who rebelled against ancient European tyrannies in 1830 and 1848. In our own century there was Tomáš Masaryk, founder of the republic of Czechoslovakia, who was well versed in the American experience. The men who made and won the American war of independence had accomplished their aim—and much, much more.

New Jersey lawyer Francis Hopkinson, agreeably talented in several fields, could dash off a poem, a drawing or a piece of music for any occasion. He was also an inventor, a close friend of Franklin, a member of Philadelphia's circle of amateur scientists. In 1777 he designed the Stars and Stripes.

James Wilson of Pennsylvania assisted in writing the Constitution and coined many golden phrases. The "Federal Republic" is his and so is the "Commonwealth of Nations" and he also invented the then expedient but now generally ignored Electoral College. Later he was named to the Supreme Court.

ARRIVING at Independence Hall, Caesar Rodney (carrying riding crop) is greeted by Delaware colleague Thomas McKean after a gallop of 80 miles to resolve a deadlock. Rodney, away hunting Tories when Congress sent for him, swung Delaware over, making the vote unanimous for independence on July 2, 1776.

Lives, fortunes—and sacred honor

IN their memories, members of the Continental Congress tended to merge the three major steps that produced the Declaration of Independence: the passage on July 2, 1776, of the resolution to declare it; the adoption on July 4 of the text proclaiming it; and the signing, begun on August 2, that solemnized it. The third step was almost an afterthought, and nearly a year elapsed before the last signature. Actually, the 56 signers popularly credited with the whole great work never met in one place at one time; a few were not even involved in the crucial vote of July 2.

Some of these men had been friends since their youth. Others had corresponded early for intercolony cooperation. The majority—at least 30—had legal training; even more were well-to-do, and almost all were experienced in public affairs. To a man, they realized that independence was an issue they had to face and resolve. They did so, in grueling sessions of open debate and closed committee work. It is the measure of their leadership that, caught in the crush of war, they reached idealistic ends by sound means out of "a decent respect to the opinions of mankind." And in pledging their "Lives . . . Fortunes, and . . . Sacred Honor," they left no doubt about their commitment to the cause.

A LIBERTY POLE is raised in celebration of the Declaration of Independence. In Philadelphia troops fired salutes "notwithstanding the shortage of powder," and "The bells rang all day and almost all night." Up in Boston "the King's Arms were . . . burnt in King Street." In Savannah joyful crowds committed "tyranny to the grave" in "a very solemn funeral procession."

The finest flower of a manor-born gentry

THE southern colonies, where support for independence was led by landed aristocrats, sent Congress two high-born representatives in Thomas Jefferson of Virginia and Charles Carroll of Carrollton, Maryland. As befitted gentlemen of their means, both had studied law, Jefferson to prepare for public life, Carroll to help in managing his many plantations. While Jefferson nourished his intellect on the works of European radicals, Carroll devoted himself to a life as graceful as his maxim for it: "Ease may be natural to a man, but elegance

—the union of propriety with ease—must be acquired."

But Carroll was no dilettante patriot. Years before hostilities began, he prophesied to an English acquaintance, "Tired of combating, in vain, against a spirit which victory after victory cannot subdue, your armies will evacuate our soil." By 1774 he was hard at work against England; he served on two Committees of Correspondence and the Maryland Committee of Safety. And although he had more to lose than any who pledged their fortunes to the cause, he signed the Declaration eagerly.

LIBERTY'S PHILOSOPHER Thomas Jefferson (*opposite*) is shown near Virginia's Natural Bridge, which he owned. An agrarian aristocrat by inheritance, he became a complete modern humanist with far-ranging interests—law, horsemanship, agriculture, botany, astronomy, invention. He designed, built and often remodeled his home, Monticello (*above*). Of his many achievements, he ranked his authorship of the Declaration first.

PATRICIAN Charles Carroll (*right*), a descendant of Irish kings, is remembered as the wealthiest man in Revolutionary America and the only Roman Catholic signer. In February 1776 he, Franklin and Samuel Chase were sent to Canada "to promote or form a union." In 1800 he retired from politics to his Maryland estates, including 10,000-acre Carrollton Manor (*above*). Outliving all other signers, he died at 95 in the railway age.

45

PEN-IN-HAND POSE of John Hancock evokes a famous story about him. Legend says he signed his name large on the Declaration so that John Bull could read it without spectacles.

Oddly assorted patriots from a hotbed of revolution

MASSACHUSETTS' five delegates to Congress were a strange mixture of political bedfellows. Robert Treat Paine was a rock of dignified conservatism. Samuel Adams, the old master agitator, was out of his element now, and he and his youthful colleague Elbridge Gerry remained in the background. It was John Adams, working day and night on major committees, who made his delegation a driving force toward independence.

John Hancock was the last, and certainly the most unpredictable, of Massachusetts' delegates. This flamboyant heir to Boston's largest shipping firm was notorious for straddling on issues up to the moment of vote. Even worse, his vanity pushed him to ludicrous extremes. He changed sides to avenge a slight, formed unsavory alliances to satisfy his need for personal glory. He devoted endless energies to wangling a commission as major general in the militia, wrote a stream of haranguing letters to get two warships on Boston ways (one named *Hancock*) launched before those being built in other ports. Yet he did a creditable job in the difficult, frustrating post of president of Congress, and he retained to the very last a strong following among the ordinary citizens.

PEACEFUL FARM in Quincy is the ancestral home of the eminent Adams line. Two Presidents were born here, John in the house at right, his son John Quincy in the "salt-box" at left.

"THE ATLAS OF INDEPENDENCE," John Adams (*opposite*) is elegantly attired as minister to England. After his return to America in 1788, Adams was elected the first Vice President.

A TALENTED COUPLE, Benjamin Rush and Julia Stockton Rush appear in portraits painted shortly after their marriage on January 11, 1777. In that year Rush served as army surgeon general and resigned after a tiff with George Washington. After the Revolution ended, Rush set up America's first free clinic, worked heroically through a yellow fever epidemic, and became the best-known doctor and medical teacher in the country.

The college at Princeton is shown as it looked about 1760. The home of college president John Witherspoon stands at the right. At center is

An intimate circle
of middle-colony comrades

CALVINIST AUSTERITY marks John Witherspoon, the only clergyman to sign the Declaration. His dignity and persuasive Scots burr made him a power in congressional committees.

FROM Pennsylvania and New Jersey, scenes of bloody clashes between Tories and patriots, came three signers who were closely knit in both their personal lives and their work for independence. This little group, centered on the college at Princeton *(below)*, included Richard Stockton, a wealthy Princeton lawyer; the Reverend John Witherspoon, able president of the college; and Dr. Benjamin Rush, an engaging Philadelphian whose interests were as numerous as Jefferson's and who pursued them "like an arrow shot from a bow."

As a student at Princeton, Rush was acquainted with college trustee Stockton. They met once again in 1767, when Rush was studying medicine at Edinburgh and Stockton arrived to offer the presidency of Princeton to Scotsman Witherspoon, a noted theologian. Witherspoon's wife was reluctant to move to the colonies, but Rush and Stockton won her over. Ten years later, while Witherspoon was deeply involved in the affairs of the college, Congress and the Presbyterian church, he was called upon to perform a wedding. The groom was Benjamin Rush; the bride was Stockton's daughter Julia.

Nassau Hall, largest building in the colonies, where Congress was meeting when it received news of the treaty which ended the Revolution.

Robert Morris' "Lemon Hill" estate, famed for its elegant hospitality, overlooks the Schuylkill River in Fairmount Park, Philadelphia.

BRILLIANT IMPROVISER Robert Morris appears stolid in this portrait but was known as a charming, dynamic man. George Washington called Morris "the financier of the Revolution."

A great lord of finance and a humble village cobbler

CONGRESSMEN Robert Morris of Pennsylvania and Roger Sherman of Connecticut were as dramatically dissimilar as any two signers. "A plain man of slender education," Sherman first worked as a shoemaker; later, as lawyer, judge and successful merchant, he remained humble, pious and "honest as an angel." A tireless committeeman, he became the only man to sign all four great documents that formed the Republic—the Articles of Association, the Declaration of Independence, the Articles of Confederation and the Constitution.

While Sherman prospered, fortune ran in reverse for Robert Morris. This shipping and banking tycoon performed prodigies to keep the army supplied. But he turned his brilliance to "dazzling the public eye by the same piece of coin, multiplied by a thousand reflectors," and finally his speculation in western land collapsed, dragging many down to ruin with him. In 1798, after months of holding off creditors at his Lemon Hill estate, he was hauled off to debtors' prison in Philadelphia.

A SOMBER MERCHANT, Roger Sherman reveals some of the awkwardness that made his contemporaries smile. His mien and dress in this portrait bespeak his Puritan upbringing. By 1772 Sherman was devoting so much time to public affairs that he was forced to retire from business. His many offices included deacon, judge, mayor of New Haven and trustee of Yale.

Trumbull's "Declaration of Independence" shows the Continental Congress convening to separate the "thirteen united States" from

The lengthening legacy of a mighty document

THE Declaration of Independence planted a rich, slow-growing harvest. From the 56 signers came two Presidents (Adams and Jefferson), three Vice Presidents (Adams, Jefferson and Gerry), 10 U.S. congressmen, 19 illustrious jurists, 16 governors and dozens of other high officeholders. As a political act, the Declaration was warmly received in France. Its lofty principles, together with America's great victory at Saratoga in October 1777, weighed heavily in the French decision to come to America's aid. As a physical document, the Declaration attracted little interest at first. Before it was fully signed, the parchment scroll began its long and often headlong travels as a casual part of Congress' baggage. After stops in Baltimore, in Lancaster and York, Pennsylvania, in Princeton, Trenton, Annapolis and New York, it finally reached Washington in 1800. Two decades later the document was being argued over, sold in facsimile and visited as an object of national pride. Ever since, its ideals have served other new nations as a foundation for their statements of national purpose.

England. The 48 men in the picture, only 43 of whom actually signed the Declaration, are identified below. Trumbull painted 36 from life.

VOTARIES OF INDEPENDENCE, JULY 4, 1776

1	WYTHE	17	R. MORRIS	33	R. LIVINGSTON
2	WHIPPLE	18	WILLING	34	JEFFERSON
3	BARTLETT	19	RUSH	35	FRANKLIN
4	LYNCH	20	GERRY	36	NELSON
5	HARRISON	21	R. T. PAINE	37	LEWIS
6	R. H. LEE	22	HOPKINS	38	WITHERSPOON
7	S. ADAMS	23	ELLERY	39	HUNTINGTON
8	CLINTON	24	CLYMER	40	WILLIAMS
9	PACA	25	HOOPER	41	WOLCOTT
10	CHASE	26	HEWES	42	THOMSON
11	STOCKTON	27	WALTON	43	HANCOCK
12	L. MORRIS	28	WILSON	44	READ
13	FLOYD	29	CLARK	45	DICKINSON
14	MIDDLETON	30	HOPKINSON	46	RUTLEDGE
15	HEYWARD	31	J. ADAMS	47	McKEAN
16	CARROLL	32	SHERMAN	48	P. LIVINGSTON

53

3. THE TURNING POINTS

A CASE could be made for the theory that America won the Revolution between Christmas night of 1776 and the opening days of the new year. True, independence was not to be achieved for another five years of harsh fighting. But American victories at Trenton and Princeton at the end of 1776 and the beginning of 1777 were to provide the first of two important turning points. Even Lord George Germain admitted that "all our hopes were blasted by that unhappy affair at Trenton." The second turning point was to come after the British surrender at Saratoga, when France openly joined the war on the side of America; at that moment the world's balance of power was altered, and with it the course of the war.

The rout at New York and the American retreat across New Jersey had seemed to offer the British a quick chance to end the rebellion. Nathanael Greene had written of the capture of Fort Washington in Manhattan: "Its consequences are justly to be dreaded." This was no exaggeration. To avoid entrapment by the pursuing British, Washington ordered a general withdrawal of his force to the south. "The rebels fled like scared rabbits," one British officer contemptuously observed.

It was part of Washington's plan to make the British complacent. He wrote on November 30, "I shall continue to retreat before them so as to lull them into security." But Congress was unnerved by the enemy's sweep across New Jersey. Anticipating the imminent capture of Philadelphia, Congress moved

SURRENDER AT TRENTON, by John Trumbull, depicts the dying Hessian commander meeting Washington. Lying wounded at left is a future President, James Monroe.

to Baltimore. Confidence in the government and the army was at ebb tide. Save for the brief rally at Harlem Heights, the American army for months had known only defeat and retreat.

Washington's tactics were generally criticized. "A certain great man is most damnably deficient" was the caustic comment of General Charles Lee. (Lee was captured under humiliating circumstances the very day he made this comment, when Banastre Tarleton surprised him, half-dressed, in a tavern where he had gone for a comfortable night's lodging.) But at this darkest moment of the war, Tom Paine heartened Americans with the eloquent words of the first of several pamphlets he entitled "The Crisis": "These are the times that try men's souls. The summer soldier and the sunshine patriot will, in this crisis, shrink from the service of their country; but he that stands it *now* deserves the love and thanks of man and woman."

In mid-December the British went into snug winter quarters, unconcerned about the American troops who had withdrawn across the Delaware River to Pennsylvania. Though Howe's forces were spread very thin across New Jersey, he did not fear the frozen and famished rebel band. But Washington, realizing that many of his troops had not re-enlisted and that their service would end on December 31, decided in desperation to strike a blow at once while he still had the manpower. His objective was the Hessian garrison at Trenton. On a stormy Christmas night, in an event romanticized by Leutze's familiar painting, Washington and his men crossed the Delaware, ferried once again by Glover's Marbleheaders. Dividing his force in two, he advanced both wings early in the morning of the 26th, through a violent snow and hailstorm. The Hessians, still sleeping off the effects of their Christmas festivities, were caught unaware by the simultaneous attack from two sides. After less than an hour of fighting, nearly the entire force was either killed or captured. The

NEW JERSEY TRIUMPHS:

WINTER, 1776-1777

To regain the initiative, Washington left his Pennsylvania winter quarters on Christmas Day, 1776, crossed the icy Delaware and overwhelmed the Hessians at Trenton. Then he returned to Pennsylvania (dotted line). But Americans, arriving by way of Bordentown too late to fight, were endangered near Trenton. Washington recrossed the Delaware to relieve them and was pinned against the river by Cornwallis, who had come rushing down from New York (brown line). Washington slipped boldly past Cornwallis and crushed the British rear guard at Princeton.

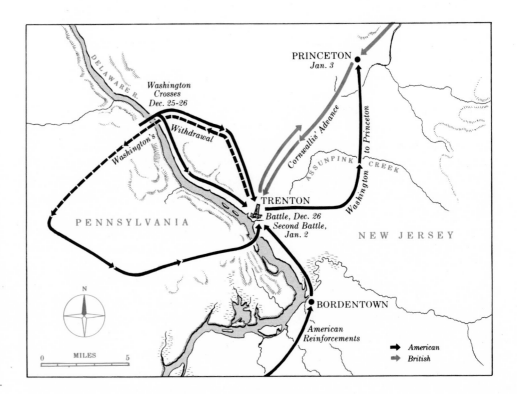

patriots suffered six casualties—two men frozen to death on the march, two officers and two privates wounded. One of the casualties was Lieutenant James Monroe.

Cornwallis, about to sail for England, rushed down from New York with heavy reinforcements. Reaching Trenton on January 2, 1777, he was urged to attack at once but said he could just as well finish the job the next morning. Washington slipped away from his camp that night and marched in darkness to Princeton, where he smashed the relatively small British garrison and seized desperately needed stores. He blasted surviving redcoats holed up in Nassau Hall and then withdrew his troops into winter quarters in the hills around Morristown.

Trenton and Princeton cleared the enemy out of nearly all of New Jersey, and their effect in restoring the patriots' shattered spirit was incalculable. The British could no longer dismiss them as a rabble in arms; "they are now become a formidable enemy" was one officer's sober appraisal.

A swashbuckling hero of many foreign wars, English-born General Charles Lee could outcurse and outsoldier any man in the Continental army. But popularity puffed up his vanity, and ambition made him insubordinate to Washington, even treasonous. He was dismissed from the service in 1780.

T HE second turning point of the war came later that year. British planners put forward an ambitious revision of the Howe-Carleton double attack which Arnold had thwarted at Valcour Bay in 1776. General Burgoyne proposed a three-pronged attack to isolate New England. The main army of not less than 8,000 regulars would push southward from Canada down Lake Champlain and the upper Hudson. An auxiliary force would thrust from Oswego eastward through the Mohawk Valley, while Howe was to send a force up the Hudson. The plan envisioned a meeting of Burgoyne and Howe at Albany, and George III had made this clear in the instructions he personally wrote out. But Howe had plans of his own. He felt he could capture Philadelphia, a seat of strong Loyalist sentiment, and still be able to spare troops, if necessary, to join the other forces at Albany. Lord George Germain ineptly approved both Burgoyne's and Howe's plans. Before he left Canada, Burgoyne knew that Howe intended to take Philadelphia before turning north to join him. He pushed on anyhow—and it was not until he was south of the Canadian border that he learned Howe probably would not meet him at all.

In early June, Burgoyne moved from St. Johns, Canada, to Lake Champlain, cautioning his Indian allies to conduct humane warfare. Edmund Burke in the Commons compared this admonition to a zoo keeper who opens the cages of his wild beasts and says: "My gentle lions—my humane bears—my tenderhearted hyenas, go forth! But I exhort you, as you are Christians and members of civil society, to take care not to hurt any man, woman or child!" Moreover, Burgoyne coupled his admonition with a warning to the patriots, the "wilful outcasts," whom he threatened with devastation and famine. Significantly, atrocities by Burgoyne's Indians did more to arouse the countryside against the British than did any patriot efforts in this area, which had been largely Tory in its sympathies.

Burgoyne, sailing south on Champlain, forced the Americans to evacuate the key fortress of Ticonderoga early in July. The loss was so shocking that Schuyler, in command of the northern army, was replaced by Horatio Gates. (Schuyler later demanded a court-martial, which cleared him of blame.) All that Alexander Hamilton, Washington's young military aide, could hope was that Burgoyne would now become overconfident and that his "enterprising spirit" might well "be fanned by his vanity into rashness."

The British force of regulars, Hessians, Loyalists and Indians, advancing from Oswego under St. Leger, laid siege to Fort Stanwix on the Mohawk River on August 3. Two patriot relief expeditions were dispatched. The first, under a German upstate landlord, General Nicholas Herkimer, was ambushed at Oriskany, but Herkimer managed to fight his way out of a trap with the loss of half his men. The second, headed by Benedict Arnold, used a ruse to frighten off St. Leger's Indians and compelled the weakened British force to retreat to Oswego. Thus one arm of Burgoyne's attack force was amputated. Another was cut off on August 16 at Bennington, where John Stark and some 2,000 raw militiamen caught Hessian Lieutenant Colonel Baum's detachment of over 700 men on a mission to seize patriot military stores and horses. Baum was fatally wounded, and almost his entire force killed or taken prisoner. Reinforcements for Baum, which arrived too late to affect the results, were also cut to pieces by Stark.

Despite the increasingly serious nature of Burgoyne's position, he pushed south toward Albany to effect the badly needed junction with the British forces from New York. Then the patriots carried Mount Defiance, neutralizing Fort Ticonderoga and threatening Burgoyne's line of possible retreat through Lake Champlain. On October 3, Clinton finally started up the Hudson. He burned Esopus (present-day Kingston) and captured two nearby forts that dominated the river. But ever cautious, Clinton went no farther toward Burgoyne and returned to New York City.

WHILE disaster faced the British army of the North, Howe persisted in his pointless Pennsylvania campaign. He left New York, sailed up Chesapeake Bay and, outflanking Washington at Brandywine on September 11, entered Philadelphia some two weeks later. On October 4 Washington counterattacked the main British army at Germantown; but the American troops lost their chance for victory by botching a pincer movement, and American detachments, lost in a heavy fog, fired upon each other. Though Washington had lost Philadelphia, his stubborn resistance threw off Howe's timetable and made it impossible for the British commander to relieve Burgoyne. Instead, Howe took a defensive posture in Philadelphia. There his troops remained until his successor, Sir Henry Clinton, left nine months later, in June 1778, to avoid a possible entrapment by the French fleet. This withdrawal was a staggering blow to the Philadelphia Loyalists, whose wholehearted collaboration with the British had exposed them to retribution by the patriots.

By early September, 1777, realizing that Howe could not come to his aid and that Clinton might not, Burgoyne had no alternative but to try to smash his way toward the south and safety. He crossed to the west side of the Hudson and moved against the entrenched position held by Gates and more than 7,000 men on Bemis Heights. On September 19 Burgoyne attempted to gain high ground on the American left, but was checked short of his goal by a force commanded by Benedict Arnold, who found a weak spot in the British line. Gates called a halt and Arnold had to stop short of a smashing victory.

On October 7 Burgoyne, making a last desperate reconnaissance in force, ventured out of his lines. American riflemen picked off the light infantry on Burgoyne's right and the grenadiers on the British left. But the decisive fighting took place in the center. Arnold, who had been removed from his command by Gates, defied Gates by leading Connecticut soldiers in a frontal

Colonel John Stark, a veteran campaigner of the French and Indian War, resigned his commission because Congress promoted junior colonels over his head. Then, with a brigade of New Hampshire militia he recruited himself, he routed 1,400 Hessians at Bennington and was finally appointed a brigadier.

assault. The British were thrown back, and Arnold then took a key redoubt. Burgoyne retreated over muddy terrain made worse by a heavy downpour to what is known today as Schuylerville, near Saratoga. Here he took his stand in prepared defense works. But his miseries increased. The army's morale was shattered, for "the commissaries had forgotten to distribute provisions" during the retreat. And the Americans "swarmed around . . . like birds of prey." Outnumbered and surrounded, Burgoyne had no choice but to surrender. On the morning of October 17, the disarmed British marched through the American camp where all was "mute astonishment and pity."

Three days after Burgoyne agreed to the surrender of Saratoga, the exultant Gates wrote his wife: "If old England is not by this lesson taught humility, then she is an obstinate old slut, bent upon her ruin." Lord North might well have agreed; he asked the king for permission to resign. But the king, rather than see the government turned over to his old enemy, the Earl of Chatham (William Pitt), pressed North to stay on. George III had his way. There was much opposition to North in Parliament, but this alone was not sufficient to bring down the ministry. And the opposition was by no means united. One of its factions wanted an end to the war; it argued for a kind of "federal union" with America, but was even prepared to recognize independence. Although Chatham also opposed the government, he found the strain of the approaching dismemberment of the empire he had built too great to bear and was carried from the House of Lords a dying man.

Something had to be done to meet the opposition at least part way and to end the American war before the French came in. The Carlisle Peace Commission, hastily dispatched to America, was empowered to negotiate with Congress, to agree if necessary to the suspension of all the obnoxious acts passed since 1763 and, in fact, to concede everything but overt independence.

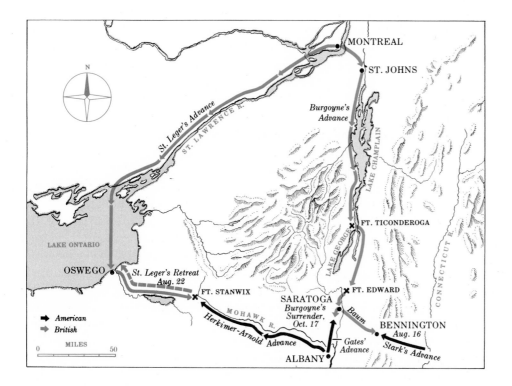

THE NORTHERN FRONT:

JUNE-OCTOBER, 1777

In 1777 the British launched two armies from Canada, hoping to take Albany and thus cut off New England from the other colonies. St. Leger, attacking from the west, besieged Fort Stanwix, but was driven back by Arnold's Americans (black line). Burgoyne, pressing south to meet St. Leger at Albany, was left with his western flank exposed. Then a Hessian detachment commanded by Friedrich Baum was smashed by John Stark at Bennington. Threatened from all sides, Burgoyne tried to fight free at Saratoga, but had to surrender to General Gates on October 17.

But the timing of the peace move was ludicrous. Fearing an attack by the French navy, Clinton pulled out of Philadelphia in June 1778, just after the British commissioners had landed. Clinton thus destroyed the bargaining position of the commission. Congress, once again in the Quaker City, refused to consider any terms less than the withdrawal of British troops and the recognition of independence. The commissioners returned to England, their mission a total failure. It is interesting to speculate what would have happened if the brothers Howe had been given as much leeway in 1776 as the Carlisle Commission had in 1778.

Polish cavalryman Casimir Pulaski was an impatient man. He came to America spoiling for action, complained to Congress whenever there was none, and earned a reputation as an unreliable malcontent. But he redeemed his name, and lost his life, while leading a headlong charge at the siege of Savannah.

Polish idealist Thaddeus Kosciuszko borrowed his fare to America and made immediate use of his artillery and engineering skills. He drew up plans for the fortification of West Point and strongholds along the Delaware River. His advice to fortify Bemis Heights sealed the British defeat near Saratoga.

Fᴏʟʟᴏᴡɪɴɢ the victory at Saratoga, France joined the war on the American side to forestall the danger that England might now conciliate the rebels. French aid had been solicited by the patriots very early in the war, although John Adams, who felt that France was bound to enter in any event, advised against a military alliance. In November 1775, Congress had set up a five-man Committee of Secret Correspondence to make contacts with "our friends" abroad. Almost at once, Benjamin Franklin, one of the committee's members, had begun to explore the possibility of foreign aid or even an alliance. French diplomats had even considered encouraging revolt by the colonies before the Revolution broke out. For it had become a cardinal point in French foreign policy that disaffection in America would weaken British power, so grossly inflated at France's expense in the Seven Years' War.

When Louis XVI had ascended the throne in 1774, he chose as his foreign minister Charles Gravier, Count de Vergennes, an experienced diplomat. Vergennes' policy of aid to America was immensely helped by an extraordinary adventurer and master of backstairs intrigue, the talented playwright Beaumarchais, who wrote *The Barber of Seville* and *The Marriage of Figaro*. In the fall of 1775 Beaumarchais and Arthur Lee of Virginia devised a plan to set up a private company to supply powder and munitions to the patriots. Although Lee, then resident in England, was authorized by Congress to learn the sentiments of foreign governments, he had no power to negotiate. So the details were ironed out in the summer of 1776, when energetic Silas Deane of Connecticut arrived in Paris to buy supplies for Congress. Beaumarchais' company was secretly and substantially subsidized by the kings of France and Spain. In September Franklin and Arthur Lee were named by Congress to join Deane as members of a diplomatic mission to France.

Aside from procuring munitions and supplies, the American envoys recruited many French and other European officers, including the Marquis de Lafayette, a gallant young aristocrat who quickly was to prove his mettle at Brandywine; the French engineer Colonel Louis Duportail; Polish volunteers like General Thaddeus Kosciuszko and Count Casimir Pulaski. One of the most important recuits was the efficient Prussian drillmaster, Baron Friedrich von Steuben. Speaking a unique mixture of French, English and German, the harassed Von Steuben gave vent to such outbursts as "Sacré! Goddam de gaucheries of dese badauts! Je ne puis plus. I can curse dem no more!" But by the spring of 1778, the Prussian officer's combination of gifted swearing and exemplary patience had turned Washington's ragged army into a disciplined fighting force.

Perhaps France would have come into the war regardless of the personality of the American envoy to the Court of Versailles, but the selection of Franklin was a stroke of pure inspiration. With his international prestige as scientist and sage, and his rare tact and diplomacy, Franklin quickly overshadowed his less gifted colleagues. Genuinely appreciative of the enormous importance of French money and supplies to the continued resistance of the patriots, Franklin used his unique talents as a propagandist to win friends for America abroad and his exceptional skills as a diplomat to forge the grand alliance. And after Saratoga, Vergennes needed little prodding. "The power that will first recognize the independence of the Americans will be the one that will reap the fruits of the war," he wrote. Pressed by the American commissioners, and without previous notice to their ally Spain, the French on January 7, 1778, approved in principle a treaty of amity and commerce and a treaty of alliance with the United States. The latter contained two significant clauses. Each of the Allies agreed to guarantee to the other the possessions in America that each might hold at the end of the war. Hence France was bound to defend the territory of the United States in continental North America, and the United States was bound to come to the defense of the French West Indies. Perhaps more immediately important, the treaty stipulated that neither party should sign a separate peace with the common enemy without the consent of the other. Both of these stipulations were a source of later difficulties.

With the French alliance a grim reality and the peace mission a fiasco, England now made desperate efforts to keep Spain from joining France. The king of Spain, Charles III, and his principal minister, Count de Floridablanca, recognized that the revolution in America might provide a dangerous example for Spain's colonies in the New World and feared American expansionism would be principally at Spain's cost. Despite the patient efforts of John Jay, for two long years the American commissioner at Madrid, Spain flatly refused to recognize the United States or provide substantial aid. Jay's persistence annoyed Floridablanca, who caustically summed up the American's twin objectives as "Spain, recognize our independence; Spain, give us more money." Even when Spain came into the war on the side of France in 1779 because England stubbornly refused to cede Gibraltar, the Spanish king carefully avoided stipulating that Spain was fighting for the independence of the United States. Actually, Spanish participation was more a liability than an asset to the American cause. As an instance, France had to divert naval strength to assist Spain's blockade of Gibraltar, which Spain had not been able to capture from England on its own. Moreover, Spain sought frantically to frustrate America's territorial ambitions beyond the Alleghenies.

THE commissioners of Congress courted rebuff by seeking recognition at European courts where their presence was unwelcome. Franklin thought it unwise to send missions to countries without any advance indication that such envoys would be acceptable. "A virgin state," he dryly observed, "should preserve its virgin character and not go about suitoring for alliances, but wait with decent dignity for the application of others."

Aside from France, America's only successful diplomatic effort was achieved in Holland. An immense military trade had grown up between the Dutch West Indian island of St. Eustatius and the United States. In retaliation, England declared war upon Holland late in 1780 and, with a few swift moves, the British smashed Dutch shipping, seized Dutch possessions in the East Indies and ended Dutch trade with the patriots. Nonetheless, in 1782 John Adams

The Marquis de Lafayette was 19 when he arrived in America. At first the British mocked him as the "stripling Frenchman." But he soon proved a skillful and valiant officer; and when a group of mutinous generals conspired to replace Washington, Lafayette supported the man who treated him as a son.

Baron von Steuben, once an aide to Frederick the Great, drilled a rabble into an army, and more. He shared in the hardships of Valley Forge, helped halt the retreat at Monmouth, and commanded the trenches at Yorktown. Congress rewarded his service, but not with the lump sum that Steuben wished.

culminated his shrewd diplomacy with a substantial loan, recognition as minister plenipotentiary, and a treaty of commerce and friendship.

Though England made a better showing against European foes than against America, these new enemies, with their world interests, forced England to scatter its naval strength from the West Indies to the Indian Ocean. To prevent a Franco-Spanish invasion which never materialized, England had to keep some ships in home waters and dispatch others to relieve Gibraltar. These naval diversions prevented England from mounting against America the kind of combined operation that might still have smashed resistance.

However, England never used its superior navy as effectively as it might against the Americans. Hampered by venality at the top, the navy was at first assigned to support amphibious operations against the insurgents. A tight blockade, imposed at the start, might have proved decisive; but the little American squadron, too weak to operate as a fleet—and the many privateers as well—managed to slip out to sea one by one despite overwhelming British naval superiority. The Continental and state navies inflicted damage to British shipping, but the privateers accounted for three times the total British shipping losses credited to the Continental navy *(see page 90)*.

Once France entered the war, American naval vessels as well as privateers could openly use French ports to harass British shipping. Hitherto they had been restrained by French fear of outraging British opinion. Now John Paul Jones could raid Whitehaven in the spring of 1778 and make a daring cruise all around the British Isles in 1779 to prove that English shipping and port facilities were open to attack. There were no big fleet engagements between the Americans and the British, but there were spectacular exploits like the three-hour battle between Jones's *Bonhomme Richard* and the *Serapis*, and Captain John Barry's stunning capture of many valuable ships.

Nor did the French and the Spanish have much to crow about. Count d'Estaing and his French ships arrived too late to intercept the British evacuation of Philadelphia; Franco-American amphibious expeditions at Newport and Savannah were ineptly managed in 1778 and 1779 respectively; and the Spanish were unable to prevent Lord Howe from coming to the relief of Gibraltar. De Grasse proved the exception: his naval support clinched the Franco-American victory at Yorktown.

THE war at sea involved relatively small numbers of seamen in each engagement. By contrast, the fighting in the back country of America was literally a matter of life and death for everyone in the area—soldiers and civilians, men and women, young and old. Yet this savage struggle in the forests settled none of the great territorial issues which were to be determined by the peace treaty. Throughout the Revolution, Indian warfare posed a threat along the western borders. Although the Indians were tied to Britain by the need to protect their hunting lands against the advancing settlers, and by trade goods, supplies and posts, the British failed to use the Indians effectively. Coordinated British attacks on the American seaports and the back country might well have been irresistible. But the British had no master plan. Their use of the Indians—undependable allies at best—antagonized liberals in England and turned neutral frontiersmen into implacable enemies.

The frontier was in almost constant terror. In the summer of 1778, Colonel John Butler and his Indian allies put to the torch the Wyoming settlements

Molly Pitcher, who was actually named Mary Ludwig Hays, is depicted at her legendary stint as a gunner. It is true Molly was the heroine of Monmouth, where she earned the sobriquet "Pitcher" by carrying water to embattled troops, but she probably did not man her husband's cannon. Another heroine, Margaret Corbin, did just that at besieged Fort Washington.

on the banks of the Susquehanna. Not long afterward, Joseph Brant, the Indian leader, and Captain Walter Butler fell upon the frontier settlement of Cherry Valley near Lake Otsego and massacred many of its inhabitants, including women and children. Sporadic attacks on patriot settlements in the Mohawk and Schoharie Valleys spread fear and horror throughout the New York and Pennsylvania borderlands, so Washington ordered a counteroffensive. Led by General Sullivan, the three-pronged invasion in the spring of 1779 cleared the Indians out of the Susquehanna, the Mohawk and Allegheny Valleys, but their striking power was unbroken. The following year the British resumed the offensive when Sir John Johnson advanced along Lake Champlain and destroyed Johnstown. Together with Brant he ravaged the Mohawk and Schoharie Valley settlements at will. Again in 1781 the Loyalists and their Indian allies spread death and destruction until Colonel Marinus Willett pushed them back to the gates of Oswego.

Americans surge uphill to recapture Stony Point, key to the lower Hudson valley. The attack, based on daring espionage by Captain Allan McLane, came at midnight on July 17, 1779. To insure stealth and surprise, Anthony Wayne ordered most of his 1,350 troops to charge with their guns unloaded. The British gave way at the point of brandished American bayonets.

FAR away, in the Old Northwest, another sort of frontier campaign took place. The conquest of the Old Northwest is almost entirely the story of George Rogers Clark, a 25-year-old surveyor and Indian fighter. It was on his initiative that in 1777 Virginia authorized an offensive designed to save Kentucky's frontier settlements from British-inspired Indian attacks. Kaskaskia surrendered without a struggle to Clark's tiny force of 175 men in July 1778. Cahokia and Vincennes also capitulated, but that winter Lieutenant Governor Hamilton (he was called "Hair Buyer" because of the bounties he paid Indians for American scalps) swept down from Detroit with an army of some 700 Indians, regulars and Canadians, and recaptured Vincennes. In an epic march of 18 days covering 180 miles across flooded prairies and treacherous swamps, Clark's small band reached Vincennes, forced the surrender of Hamilton's garrison and made the "Hair Buyer" prisoner. But Clark's force was too small to push on to Detroit, which, together with Forts Niagara, Oswego and Michilimackinac, the British still held at the war's end. Despite Clark's exploits, he was unable to protect Kentucky from vicious raids or to provide a solid basis of occupation to support America's claim to the western lands at the peacemaking. Demand for the western lands had to rest on colonial charter rights; it may truly be said that the West was won by bold diplomacy rather than by colorful military feats.

Every one of these campaigns, major or minor, required the bare military necessities of guns, clothing and food. At times, lacking these essentials, the colonial army threatened to fall apart. Presumably, these tools and provisions of war were to be furnished by the states or by Congress. But the states could not be depended upon, and Congress lacked strong fiscal powers. This constitutional deficiency imperiled the war effort and encouraged inflation and bankruptcy. Indeed, paper money was more to be feared than British generals.

Money was the fuel that kept the machinery of war running. American finances disintegrated rapidly after 1779 despite subsidies and loans (largely contributed by France, a small part from Spain) totaling for the entire period of the war almost nine million dollars. By the beginning of 1780 Congress had issued nearly $250 million in paper money (Continentals) and had incurred immense additional obligations in the form of quartermaster certificates for supplies, guarantees for private loans and certificates given to the soldiers for back pay. And over $200 million in paper money was issued by the states

This navy flag, used by John Paul Jones, was one of several early American flags that bore a rattlesnake and the motto "Don't tread on me." Each of the 13 colonies had its own banner until the Grand Union flag, which featured stripes and crosses, was put on display by George Washington in 1776.

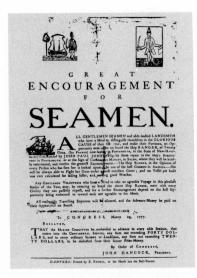

This poster called for "Gentlemen Volunteers" to serve aboard John Paul Jones's "Ranger," bound for France in 1777. Seamen received a share in prize money—one half the value of captured men-of-war, one third the value of merchant-men. They shopped for the best ship, enlisted for one cruise only.

despite the protests of Congress. By early 1779 eight paper dollars were worth one dollar in metal coin, but by the end of the year the ratio had fallen to 40 to 1.

To stem the ruinous tide, Congress adopted spartan measures. In 1780 it resolved to reduce the bills in circulation by accepting them in payments due it from the states at one fortieth of their face value. In 1781 Robert Morris was named Superintendent of Finance. Supported in his efforts by a timely subsidy from France and a large loan from the Netherlands, Morris sponsored a national bank and reformed the army's inefficient purchasing system.

Congress and the states realized that unless the cost of operating the war could be kept down, the nation would go bankrupt. On the eve of hostilities Congress had not only imposed nonimportation regulations but had fixed limits to hold the line on prices of goods already imported. Toward the close of '76 the New England states took joint action to set maximum price and wage ceilings. But one region could not hold the price line when it was not observed elsewhere, and the war years were marked by a rapid rise in the cost of living and an orgy of profiteering.

Congress sidestepped the issue, and the precipitate decline in the value of paper money prompted constant revisions of regional, state and local price schedules by state legislatures and interstate conventions. The methods of enforcement—boycott, social ostracism and mob fury, rather than legal action—did not work. The failure of price controls stemmed directly from the inability of Congress and the states to stabilize the currency and from their preference for inflation over a program of realistic taxation.

WHILE profiteers waxed fat, fighting men shivered and starved, both at Valley Forge, Washington's headquarters west of Philadelphia during the winter of 1777-1778, and at Morristown, New Jersey, in the even severer winter of 1779-1780. "God grant we may never be brought to such a wretched condition again!" Nathanael Greene wrote of Valley Forge, which has become a symbol of courage and selfless patriotism. That Washington's army, famished, ragged and ill, miraculously survived the ordeals of these winter encampments was no tribute to Congress or to the merchant speculators, both of which were responsible for provisioning and supplies. To critics of his winter strategy Washington retorted, "It is a much easier and less distressing thing to draw remonstrances in a comfortable room by a good fireside than to occupy a cold bleak hill and sleep under frost and snow without cloaths or blankets."

Washington, ordinarily a very temperate man, expressed himself violently on the need for stern measures to crush that "abominable lust of gain" which sought to capitalize on the desperate needs of fighting men. "I would to God," he wrote in 1778, "that one of the most attrocious [speculators] of each State was hung in gibbets upon a gallows five times as high as the one prepared by Haman. No punishment in my opinion," he added, "is too great for the man who can build his greatness upon his country's ruin." On October 4, 1779, a mob of militiamen attacked the Philadelphia residence of James Wilson, a patriot lawyer who had incurred the special animosity of the radicals because of his association with profiteers. Moreover, Wilson's own speculations were notorious. He and a group of fellow speculators barricaded themselves inside his house and prepared to shoot it out, but they were rescued by a troop of cavalry commanded in person by Joseph Reed, president of Pennsylvania's Supreme Executive Council.

The attack on "Fort Wilson" dramatically highlighted the grievances of men in uniform, whether militia or Continental troops. Many were in rags, reduced to bread and water and forced to go for months without pay. It is not surprising that there were mutinies. A minor one took place in May 1780, when two Connecticut regiments demanded back pay. Pennsylvania troops were summoned, then withdrawn, while the would-be mutineers simmered down.

On the night of January 1, 1781, some 2,400 men of the Pennsylvania line, encamped in New Jersey, mutinied, chose spokesmen to present their case to Congress and forced President Reed to accede to most of their terms. This was the most serious incident of its kind, but there were others. A few weeks later, three New Jersey regiments mutinied. Washington acted swiftly to crush the mutiny, executing a few of the ringleaders on the spot.

THESE mutineers were asserting legitimate grievances in an illegitimate way, but they had no intention of joining the enemy, and the British quickly found that the army could not be seduced from its allegiance. Yet if treason did not contaminate the rank and file, it did leave its brand on a few in places of trust. Throughout the war, Dr. Edward Bancroft, Franklin's secretary in Paris, reported to the British ministry all the plans and projects of the Americans that passed across his desk. Silas Deane, who next to Franklin did most to secure foreign aid for the patriot cause, openly turned against Congress in 1780 and later advocated making peace with England and returning to the old allegiance. But the first treachery was unknown and not disclosed for another century, and the second could be attributed to Deane's mental unbalance caused by anger at his recall by Congress because of charges brought by his enemies that he had profited by his mission.

No treachery in the whole Revolution was comparable in magnitude to that of Benedict Arnold. After his shabby treatment by Gates at Saratoga, Arnold was given command of Philadelphia, where his wild extravagance brought him a court-martial and a reprimand for improper conduct that bordered on corruption. He still retained the confidence of Washington, who gave him command of West Point. Arnold, reckless and ambitious, devoid of moral conviction and incapable of remorse, then contracted with Sir Henry Clinton to betray West Point. He put the traitorous agreement down on paper quite cold-bloodedly: his property to be secured, a substantial life annuity guaranteed and a thumping cash payment if he succeeded in turning over the garrison.

How Arnold's plans went awry, how his intermediary, Major André, was captured in civilian clothes near Tarrytown, the incriminating plans discovered and, in Nathanael Greene's words, "treason of the blackest dye" exposed is part of the folklore of the American Revolution.

The astounding revelation of Arnold's treason came at a dark moment for the patriot cause. Disheartening news had come from the lower South, where the patriot army under Horatio Gates had been routed at Camden only a few weeks before and was now fragmented and, in effect, leaderless. The shock provided by Arnold's act rallied all patriots behind Washington, and the morale of the fighting men was boosted for the critical battles ahead. Washington himself made perhaps the most judicious comment on Arnold when he sensibly observed that traitors "are the growth of every country, and in a revolution of the present nature it is more to be wondered at that the catalogue is so small than that there have been found a few."

This pass from Benedict Arnold almost took André safely through American lines. Learning that his courier to Clinton was captured, Arnold fled to New York from the garrison he betrayed, West Point. Alexander Hamilton, as Washington's aide, wrote Clinton offering the exchange of André for Arnold.

Lafayette and Washington inspect huddled American troops during the terrible winter at Valley Forge.

Grim ordeals and a taste of success

THE bloody footprints that led to snowy Valley Forge in 1777 brought dark thoughts to George Washington. He warned Congress that unless his soldiers were given decent supplies, the army "must inevitably be reduced to one or other of these three things. Starve, dissolve, or disperse. . . ." Lafayette, the ardent young Frenchman, was horrified by the Americans' plight—"They had neither coats, hats, shirts, nor shoes; their feet and legs froze until they became black. . . ." In log huts the patriots slept on lice-infested straw, and died by the hundreds from typhus. For his "Thanksgiving" dinner, each man was allowed a half gill of rice and a tablespoonful of vinegar.

Yet with all these dismal conditions the army was warmed by its growing self-confidence, and by wonderful news from the north. American morale had plummeted to its lowest point in late 1776, during the terrible retreat that followed the humiliating defeats in New York. But after victories at Trenton and Princeton, the army knew that its enemy could be beaten. And after Saratoga, it realized that Britain's major strategic effort in America had utterly failed. When it was the British turn to retreat from Philadelphia, in the early summer of 1778, the hardened veterans of Valley Forge came swarming after them.

THE MURDER OF JANE McCREA near Fort Edward, New York, in 1777 is depicted here. Jane was awaiting her lover, a Tory officer, when she was seized by Burgoyne's Indian scouts. The Indians shot and scalped her in a quarrel over who would bring her into camp. This senseless crime enraged patriots and Tories, and added hundreds of recruits to the American army.

WASHINGTON AT THE DELAWARE sits his horse before crossing. The surprise attack that followed was made possible by the tireless skill of the Yankee boatmen who ferried the army.

Turnabout at Trenton

As the year 1776 ended, a ringing triumph came to the patriots, who had so often been beaten. On Christmas night, in a storm of snow and sleet that cut "like a knife," as one man said, they pushed their boats across the icy Delaware and fell upon Howe's troops in Trenton. The surprise was complete—three Hessian regiments were smashed (nearly 1,000 men were captured) and their commander was mortally wounded. Only four Americans were wounded, but two men died from cold.

The victory was sweet to Washington, whose record up to then was largely one of defeat. Even sweeter was his satisfaction in outwitting Cornwallis and winning another sharp fight at Princeton a few days later (painting below). These successes, small in themselves but stupendous for American morale, took Washington out of the amateur class as a general. The rebels, a British officer lamented, seemed to possess "extreme cunning."

AT PRINCETON, American artillery fires while Washington prepares to lead the attack. This battle broke two British regiments, trapped 194 prisoners in Nassau Hall and forced the British to flee most of New Jersey. William Mercer, son of an American general killed in the action, painted this view of the fight.

SCENE OF A TRAP set for Washington near Assunpink Creek bridge is shown above. Smarting after Trenton, and swearing to "bag the fox," Cornwallis rushed up fresh troops and tried to pin the Americans between the creek and the Delaware. But on the night of January 2, Washington left decoy fires burning, silently moved his men to the British rear and hit at Princeton.

Charge at Bemis Heights is led by Benedict Arnold on a white horse. At right, British General Simon Fraser is carried away after being

Saratoga, end of a dream

SARATOGA ended forever the British dream of cutting the colonies in two by an invasion from Canada. The American commander, Horatio Gates, set up strong lines at Bemis Heights, close to Saratoga, and awaited Burgoyne's army there. But Arnold refused to wait; his division attacked at Freeman's Farm on September 19, 1777. Later, Gates took away Arnold's command—but Arnold stayed close to his troops. On October 7, when the two armies clashed again, Arnold suddenly appeared on the field in his general's uniform and took charge *(above)*. Arnold's aggressive courage and British overconfidence gave the Americans a spectacular victory. Burgoyne lost 1,200 troops and then surrendered 5,700 more in what turned out to be the most decisive campaign of the war.

shot by sniper Tim Murphy, in the tree at left. Arnold suffered a severe wound in his left leg, which had already been hurt at Quebec.

HESSIANS are led off *(left)* after a successful attack by Stark's militia near Bennington, Vermont, on August 16, 1777. "We'll beat them before night," Stark had vowed, "or Molly Stark will be a widow."

SURRENDER of Burgoyne to General Gates at Saratoga is seen *(right)* in this painting by Trumbull. Gates's unwise promise to send the captured British army back home was later annulled by Congress.

Treason at a high level

THE tragic sequel to Benedict Arnold's bravery came two years after Saratoga. In April of 1779 he had married Peggy Shippen, a Philadelphia society belle, and he went into debt to support her in grand style. Embittered by slights from Congress and by charges of profiteering while he was military commander of Philadelphia, Arnold turned traitor soon after. He began sending military information in secret cipher to Sir Henry Clinton, the new British commander in New York, and suggesting a price of £10,000 for his services.

In the summer of 1780, Arnold persuaded Washington to give him command of West Point, the key American defense position on the Hudson River. Then Arnold offered to surrender the fort and join the British army for £20,000. He even advised Clinton how to capture Washington. Major John André, Clinton's handsome aide—who had known Peggy Shippen in Philadelphia—went up the Hudson in uniform to coordinate plans for the surrender (left). On the way back to New York, André, now in disguise, was captured and hanged as a spy (opposite). Arnold escaped and led terror raids for the British in Virginia and his home state, Connecticut. For all his acts of treason, he received a handsome payment— £6,315—but he died in exile, despised by the British.

TRAITOR AND SPY, General Benedict Arnold (seated, above) and Major John André arrange the betrayal of West Point in September 1780. Arnold suggests hiding papers in André's stocking.

ARNOLD AND THE DEVIL—in effigy—are hauled through Philadelphia streets in a cart (above) soon after the treason plot was exposed. This woodcut shows a two-faced Arnold in a military coat being drawn toward a bonfire while Satan mocks the traitor with a bag of gold and threatens him with a pitchfork.

ANDRE'S DEATH near Tappan, New York, is shown opposite. He asked to be shot as a soldier, but Washington ordered him hanged as a spy. He bandaged his own eyes, adjusted the noose himself, and the patriots allowed him to die in his uniform. "I am," he said, "reconciled to my fate but not to the mode."

A NIGHT ATTACK by the British at Paoli *(opposite)* reaches a savage height on September 21, 1777. After suffering frightful losses, the stunned American troops under Anthony Wayne broke and fled.

A PISTOL-WHIPPING subdues a British cavalryman *(right)* as he tries to capture Captain Allan McLane, the daring patriot scout, early on June 16, 1778. McLane fought clear and rode off safe and sound.

Mayhem and massacre between the lines

WHILE the main armies fought infrequent battles, a ceaseless war of attrition went on between the cavalry scouts, raiding parties and guerrillas of both sides. Not many prisoners were taken in this kind of fighting. The British set an example of ruthlessness when their Tory spies marched them to a detached force of sleeping Americans near Paoli, Pennsylvania, during Howe's advance on Philadelphia. Rushing in with bayonets fixed they stabbed until their muscles were tired, killing or wounding some 300 patriots while losing only a handful of men. Other similar "massacres" were staged in New Jersey and Pennsylvania by the dreaded Loyalists of the Queen's Rangers, under Major John Simcoe. Even Tories were not always safe against British raiders. When Simcoe's Rangers swept down on a household at Hancock's Bridge, the Tory owners were slaughtered along with some American militia billeted there.

On the American side, the most noted raider was Captain Allan McLane of Delaware *(above, left)*, whose independent squadron of horsemen, infantry, Indians and spies screened Washington's army—and sometimes fed it—during the ordeal of Valley Forge. McLane's men specialized in seizing cattle destined for British troops in Philadelphia, and in keeping Washington informed of every British movement. Dashing along the country roads wearing beaver hats and rough hunting shirts, McLane's mounted partisans showed no mercy to British pickets or local collaborators. McLane won further glory later, when he personally spied out Stony Point's defenses before the successful American attack in 1779.

British bumbling, high jinks and a change of command

SIR WILLIAM HOWE spent the third winter of the war as he had the first two—in pursuit of cozy pleasure. He settled into the Richard Penn house on Market Street in Philadelphia, appropriated a fine coach and horses in town and attended all the balls, cockfights and plays his elegant officers could contrive. Occasionally the war ruffled Sir Billy's phlegm. In October 1777 Washington fell on Howe's main force at Germantown *(right)*. Only American confusion caused by fog on the battlefield and a too-complicated battle plan saved the British. That winter London angrily wanted to know why Howe did not attack Washington's weakened army shivering at Valley Forge, and in the spring his resignation was accepted. His officers gave him a grand farewell. By day there was a mock tournament in which seven knights of the "Blended Rose" fought seven knights of the "Burning Mountain" for the honor of 14 maidens dressed in Turkish clothes. By night there was dining, dancing and card playing and, just before dawn, fireworks ending with a figure representing "Fame" displaying in letters of fire the message "Thy laurels shall never fade." Strong soldiers wept as he left for England. Then the new commander, General Sir Henry Clinton, took the British cause in charge.

INEFFECTIVE CAMPAIGNS against the rebels rouse the British ire, as shown in this contemporary cartoon. The Howe brothers dally *(left)* over a punch bowl while foreigners despoil the cow of commerce, and British warships stand forlorn. Even the British lion, despite kicks from an angry Englishman, drowses.

On the fogbound battlefield near Germantown,

American reserves become confused and waste their energy trying to capture the Chew mansion, a stone house of little strategic importance.

77

A day saved by an angry man

His temper flaring, George Washington swears "till the leaves shook on the trees." This painting by Emanuel Leutze shows the American commander *(center, with upraised sword)* riding into the flaming melee at Monmouth Court House, New Jersey. He encountered General Charles Lee retreating instead of at-

tacking, as Washington had explicitly ordered him to do. Lee, sitting potbellied on his horse at left, could only stammer "Sir? Sir?" to Washington's angry questions. In a towering rage, Washington called Lee "a damned poltroon." Then he turned the army around and formed it in position behind a hedge to meet the British attack. The fighting that followed, on a blistering hot day, was as costly to the British as to the Americans, but both sides held their ground. That night, the British quietly made an orderly retreat, boarded ships and reached safety in New York, there to prepare for the threat of a French invasion.

4. VICTORY AND INDEPENDENCE

Between Saratoga in 1777 and Yorktown in 1781, there were times when the prospects of victory seemed bleak and forlorn even to the most steadfast patriot. The results of the alliance with France had fallen short of expectations, the American cause was haunted by the twin specters of bankruptcy and disaffection, and, late in 1778, the British for once managed to mount a tremendously powerful offensive that threatened to sever the lower South from the rest of the Confederation.

The Carolinas and Georgia constituted a stronghold of loyalism, particularly in the back country, and the British expected that winning there would be comparatively easy. After the withdrawal of the redcoats from Philadelphia in June 1778, Sir Henry Clinton was ordered to launch a campaign against the South. The British naval forces attacked the American front at the Savannah River, infantry hit the rebels from the rear, and the Americans broke in confusion. Savannah fell, then Sunbury and Augusta were taken and a royal government was re-established in Georgia.

With a formidable armada carrying a mixed force of nearly 8,000 British, Hessian and Tory soldiers, Clinton then sailed to Charleston, South Carolina, chief port of the southern states. This time Charleston offered no repetition of the successful stand that Moultrie had made in 1776 against the British invasion. The defenses of the port had been neglected, and there were not enough big guns in position to protect the harbor against the invading fleet.

THE PEACE NEGOTIATORS, painted by Benjamin West, are, from the left: John Jay, John Adams, Benjamin Franklin, Henry Laurens and their aide, Franklin's grandson William.

French Baron de Kalb lies mortally wounded on the battlefield near Camden while his aide shields him from a pack of redcoats with bayonets. De Kalb was a self-made nobleman. Because European custom was to offer commissions to aristocrats only, young Johann Kalb, son of a Bavarian peasant, promoted himself to the nobility to help further his military career.

Nonetheless, General Benjamin Lincoln, the patriot commander, withdrew into the city with nearly all his forces, some 5,000 men. He left only a small cavalry detachment at Monck's Corner, about 30 miles north of Charleston, near the head of the Cooper River, to keep open his line of communication with the northern part of the state. These isolated horsemen were quickly overrun in a predawn surprise attack by 26-year-old Lieutenant Colonel Banastre Tarleton and his green-uniformed British Legion, a Tory cavalry outfit. Then Clinton sent newly arrived reinforcements to occupy the last open stretch of ground between the Cooper River and the sea.

Lincoln capitulated on May 12, 1780. He had little choice: the American army was bottled up and civilian morale was wobbly after nine weeks of a punishing siege. The surrender of Charleston, with its enormous army of defenders, was the largest single patriot loss of the war.

THE British next moved to snuff out the last flickers of insurrection in South Carolina. What followed was savage civil war. "Bloody" Tarleton, whose name became synonymous with ruthless warfare, massacred a patriot detachment near Waxhaw Creek after their commander had asked for quarter. Rebels whipped Tories at Ramsour's Mill, with heavy casualties on both sides. Rocky Mount and Hanging Rock were scenes of obstinate fighting, and at Rocky Mount, patriot dragoons literally hacked the Tories to pieces. In the absence of regular Continental forces, patriot resistance was largely local and disorganized, kept alive by guerrilla bands led by men like Thomas Sumter, Francis Marion (the "Swamp Fox") and Andrew Pickens.

Congress decided to take a hand. Against the advice of George Washington, who preferred Nathanael Greene, the representatives gave command of the southern troops to Horatio Gates, the hero of Saratoga. "Take care lest your Northern laurels turn to Southern willows," General Charles Lee prophetically advised Gates. Gates did everything wrong. He was advised to follow a circuitous route from North Carolina to Camden, one which would take his army through prosperous and sympathetic territory. Instead he chose a shorter course through forest and marshes, where Loyalist sentiments were stronger than in almost any other part of the South. Gates forced his sick and starving men through this hostile countryside and even ordered an exhausting night march on the eve of battle.

On paper, Gates boasted an immense numerical superiority over his adversary, Lieutenant Colonel Francis, Lord Rawdon. But when Rawdon confronted Gates at Camden in August 1780, the British had been reinforced by the timely arrival of Cornwallis. Gates detached some 400 regulars and sent them to Thomas Sumter, and he also ordered Marion off on a useless mission. Gates made further mistakes in the disposition of his troops. Shortly before the armies clashed, he switched the positions of his untried militia on the left and center. The British light infantry charged almost before this reckless maneuver was completed. A stampede ensued as the militia dropped their guns and ran for their lives.

Baron de Kalb, one of the European volunteers who had arrived with Lafayette in 1777, stood his ground with a handful of regulars until he was fatally wounded. Then a combined British cavalry and foot attack broke up the last defenses. The patriot army was utterly routed and dispersed, and Gates ended his military career in flight. Riding a swift horse, he did not dismount until that night, when he was safe in Charlotte, 60 miles from the fighting.

"For God's sake overcome prejudice and send Greene," young Alexander Hamilton wrote Congressman James Duane of New York. Nathanael Greene had been passed over earlier for several reasons: he had risen from the ranks and thus lacked prestige in the eyes of certain influential congressmen, and his candor had not endeared him to others. Now, Greene's ability outweighed other considerations and he was named to replace Gates on October 14, 1780. When he reached the South, he switched from formal warfare to the guerrilla tactics of the Carolina partisans. He transferred some of his own troops to Daniel Morgan, one of the few military geniuses the war produced, and with this additional strength Morgan went off to harass British outposts in the western part of South Carolina. Greene took his troops to the north-central section to aid the guerrilla actions there.

Meantime, Cornwallis' army had bogged down in the fiercely patriot country around Charlotte, North Carolina. To cover his left flank, Cornwallis dispatched Major Patrick Ferguson's Tories into the uplands, where they burned and plundered as they advanced. But Ferguson was stalked by Colonel Isaac Shelby, who had joined forces with four other partisan commanders. These 900 patriot backwoodsmen isolated Ferguson atop King's Mountain, just south of the North Carolina boundary line, where Ferguson "defied God Almighty and all the rebels out of Hell to overcome him." Unimpressed by this blasphemy, the attackers did just that. When the Tories cried for quarter, the frontiersmen, remembering Tarleton, yelled "Tarleton's quarter!" and butchered Ferguson's men until American officers stopped the killing. The defeat of the Loyalists at King's Mountain destroyed once and for all Tory prestige in North Carolina, and forced Cornwallis to retreat south across the state line to Winnsborough.

Morgan and Greene were now 140 miles apart. Cornwallis detached Tarleton to handle the frontiersmen under Morgan, while he readied himself for battle with Greene. On January 16, 1781, Morgan's scouts reported that Tarleton, with some 1,100 regulars and Tories, would reach the Americans in a day. Lacking boats, Morgan realized that his somewhat outnumbered men could not withdraw in time across the unfordable Broad River. Although the memory of Camden still smarted, Morgan decided to fight and take the risk that his men might panic again. This time, with the river behind them, they would have no place to run.

The scene of the battle was a clearing called the Cowpens, where cows had formerly grazed. Morgan's moves were unorthodox, but his strategy made this the patriots' best-fought battle of the whole war. The raw militia were placed in the front line. Morgan exhorted them to fire just two volleys, after which they could retire. Behind them were the Continentals and some seasoned Virginia militiamen, ordered to hold their ground at all cost. To the rear, on a low ridge sheltered from British fire, Morgan placed his cavalry.

While Tarleton's men advanced to within 100 yards, Morgan pleaded with his militia: "Look for the epaulets! Pick off the epaulets!" After two volleys, which shredded the attackers, the militiamen, as agreed, retired toward the low ridge in the rear. The British bravely lunged against the next rank. As the entire American line was pulled back, Tarleton's men, already tasting victory, rushed forward. Then Morgan ordered his Virginians to charge with bayonets,

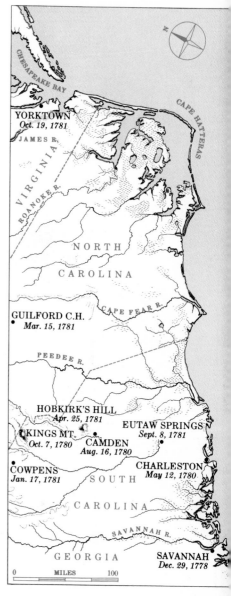

SOUTHERN CAMPAIGNS

1778-1781

Most of the battles during the last three years of the Revolution were fought in the South, over the vast territory from Georgia to Virginia. The campaigning started with the first British victory at Savannah, and in the months that followed, the principal American triumphs were on King's Mountain and at Cowpens. There were patriot defeats at Charleston, Camden and Guilford Court House. The British were the technical victors at Hobkirk's Hill and Eutaw Springs. But in the end, the Americans did so much damage that the redcoats at last withdrew to fortify Yorktown.

and routed the British. When Tarleton's dragoons tried to cover the retreat, poised American cavalrymen swooped down and stopped them. In the whole-sale British capitulation that followed, only Tarleton and a corporal's guard of his men made good their escape.

Cowpens, coming at the start of 1781, showed that the new year might make amends for the disappointments of 1780. Despite a ruthless offensive, the British had failed to subdue the South. Moreover, the main patriot army, soon heavily reinforced by French troops, posed a serious threat to the British control of cities such as New York and Charleston.

One of the Revolution's youngest generals, Nathanael Greene, son of a Quaker preacher, was expelled by the Society of Friends for his firm belief in armed resistance to the crown. Greene sold his south-ern lands to help meet the expenses of his army; at war's end, grateful Georgians voted him a plantation.

THE English people were war-weary after nearly six years of fighting. In Parliament, the Opposition was determined to overthrow Lord North's ministry and make peace even at the price of recognizing American independence. For Britain's prized supremacy on the seas was threatened by a grand alliance of France and Spain, now ready, despite mutual rivalries and suspicions, for a last supreme effort after a miserable start. And the neutral states had been mobilized by Catherine II of Russia into the League of Armed Neutrality, pledged to fight against England's harsh maritime policy and for freedom of the seas. The league, to which most of the nonbelligerents adhered, insisted on a liberal definition of noncontraband goods that would enable them to continue their trade with France and Spain, free from the threat of seizure by England's blockading navy.

For the British army in America, 1781 was a year of disaster. To avenge Cowpens, which had cost him Tarleton's light troops, Cornwallis trans-formed his whole force into light troops by destroying all superfluous baggage. They were now stripped down for sprinting. But Nathanael Greene, out-numbered 3 to 2, could sprint even faster. He made a superb withdrawal across four rivers, the Catawba, the Yadkin, the Deep and finally the Dan.

Thus for weeks Greene eluded the action that Cornwallis desperately sought. On March 15, after securing reinforcements, he finally confronted the British at Guilford Court House in North Carolina. Drawing on the battle plan of Morgan at Cowpens, Greene gave the North Carolina militia the privilege of retiring after firing two rounds. But when the British plunged forward, Greene was reluctant to risk all on the fate of a cavalry counter-attack. Then Cornwallis opened fire with artillery, using grapeshot which was both deadly and inaccurate. Many British as well as Americans were killed. Though Greene's position became untenable, the British suffered heavily. "Another such victory would destroy the British army," an Opposition states-man, Charles James Fox, ironically commented.

Both generals now withdrew: Cornwallis to Virginia to get closer to his communications bases; Greene, prudently, to the south to reconquer South Carolina and Georgia. Despite the aid of such masterly partisan warriors as Francis Marion and Andrew Pickens, Greene found the reconquest a dis-couraging and costly business. A second battle of Camden was fought on April 25 at Hobkirk's Hill. Even his battle-hardened Continentals stumbled and Greene was forced to break off the action, although the British had suffered greater casualties. "We fight, get beat, rise, and fight again," Greene wrote philosophically to the Chevalier de la Luzerne, the French envoy to Congress. Again in September, Greene fought a major engagement with Brit-ish troops under Lieutenant Colonel Alexander Stewart at Eutaw Springs

—a bloody, indecisive three-hour battle in intense heat. This time the British were decimated, and Stewart had to fall back to the vicinity of Charleston and the protection of British warships. Greene had lost his battles, but he had won his ground. For all practical purposes, the redcoats were forced to abandon the lower South.

Virginia saw the war's last major military operations. The Old Dominion, ravaged in January by raiders led by Benedict Arnold, was heartened by Washington's dispatch of the young Marquis de Lafayette with three regiments of light infantry to its defense. In April a new peril threatened when Cornwallis began his movement north from Wilmington, North Carolina. As the patriots retreated into the interior before superior numbers, the British staged daring forays, the most notable being Tarleton's wild dash to the capital at Charlottesville in June. Several members of the state legislature were caught before they could escape, but Thomas Jefferson, whose term as governor had expired two days before, just managed to elude Tarleton.

Cornwallis argued strongly for an all-out campaign to capture the whole of Virginia, but his superior officer, General Clinton, was reluctant to spare reinforcements, for he expected that the rebels might attack New York in force. Finally, Clinton agreed that Cornwallis should take up a position in Virginia and hold it. At this point, Cornwallis had little choice but to march his troops from the interior toward the Chesapeake, for he was being harried by a reinforced Lafayette who hung doggedly on his rear. Cornwallis followed Clinton's orders and fortified Yorktown and Gloucester, which were located on either side of the York River.

The elusive "Swamp Fox," General Francis Marion, was the Revolution's best guerrilla fighter. He was a small man—so tiny at birth that he "might easily have been put into a quart pot." His technique was to raid the British, then disappear swiftly into the coastal swamplands, safe from pursuit.

IN picking camps handy to the sea, Cornwallis counted on the British navy maintaining its traditional supremacy in American waters. There was nothing in the futile record of combined Franco-Spanish naval operations before 1781 to make him think otherwise. "With a naval inferiority," as Lafayette bluntly informed the French government in January of 1781, "it is impossible to make war in America." What Cornwallis did not count upon was the aggressiveness of a French admiral and the flexibility and wiliness of Washington's grand strategy. And through this miscalculation, Cornwallis, with all his experience, was to be trapped irretrievably.

At this moment, for the first time since the French entered the war, their forces could undertake a combined land-sea operation with the patriots. The French troops, which had reached Newport in July 1780, were commanded by the astute and experienced Count de Rochambeau. In the spring of 1781, a powerful fleet commanded by Count de Grasse sailed from Brest for the West Indies. The question was how the American and French forces could be used most effectively in a joint operation. Washington had good reason to be conservative in his expectations. On May 21 he conferred with Rochambeau at Wethersfield, Connecticut. They agreed on a joint attack on New York to be supported by De Grasse's fleet, but Rochambeau also gave De Grasse the option of moving against Cornwallis.

In July Rochambeau's French army joined Washington's Americans north of New York City, but a change in strategy was spurred by De Grasse's decision to sail to the Chesapeake, where, he informed Washington, he could remain no longer than October. This ruled out a New York campaign for the Americans. Accordingly, on August 17 Washington wrote the French ad-

"Big Dan" Morgan, a brilliant patriot leader, bore a personal grudge against the British for a beating he once received from an English officer. He quit the army in a huff when passed over for promotion, but relenting, left Virginia to rejoin Gates in North Carolina, selling a mare for traveling expenses.

miral: "It has been judged expedient to turn our attention toward the South."

Washington's new plan was executed with such secrecy that even his own officers were fooled. The Allied forces began crossing the Hudson on August 20 and simulated an attack on New York City through Staten Island, in the lower bay. This buttressed Clinton's conviction that Washington wanted to seize Sandy Hook to cover the entrance of the French fleet into New York harbor. Clinton had to hold his huge garrison in battle readiness, and the British naval commander, Admiral Graves, did not dare to order his fleet out of New York. It was not until the main American army had crossed the Delaware, still heading south, that it became obvious that Washington's real objective was Yorktown.

At the same time, the French fleet was adhering to its schedule. On August 30, De Grasse reached the mouth of the York River and blockaded Cornwallis. When the British fleet under Admiral Graves appeared on September 5, De Grasse sailed out to give battle. With the help of reinforcements from Newport, De Grasse managed to outsail, outshoot and outsmart the British rescue expedition, which was forced to return to New York for repairs. This naval engagement was really the decisive battle. Once he had achieved command of the seas off Yorktown, De Grasse could even dispatch ships to fetch most of Washington's 9,000 troops and Rochambeau's 7,800 down Chesapeake Bay to Williamsburg.

The Allied army took up siege positions before Yorktown on September 28. Cornwallis commanded a mixed British and German force of almost 8,000 men. Two days later Cornwallis decided to give up his outer lines, which meant that Allied siege guns could pound every yard of his inner defense works. And together, the Americans and the French formed a tight semicircle around Cornwallis.

"We have got him handsomely in a pudding bag," General George Weedon exultantly wrote Nathanael Greene. For six days in October an incessant bombardment pounded the surrounded defenders. The climax of the great siege came on October 14, with the two bayonet attacks on British redoubts near the river. One assault was led by a French lieutenant colonel, Count Guillaume de Deux-Ponts, and the other by Alexander Hamilton, long an aide to Washington and now at last given the chance for military glory on his own. A British counterattack two days later failed to regain these key points. In desperation Cornwallis planned a night escape by water across the York River, but a sudden storm halted the project.

O N October 20 Cornwallis wrote Clinton: "I have the mortification to inform your Excellency that I have been forced to give up the posts of York and Gloucester, and to surrender the troops under my command." Thus tersely did a British general inform his superior of the greatest military defeat Britain had suffered in many generations. On October 19, at 2 p.m., the British and German troops had marched out in front of their posts. The combined Allied armies were drawn up in two lines extending more than a mile in length. On the right side of the road, in motley array, some even without uniforms, were the ragged patriot troops headed by Washington on horseback. The French, resplendent in military attire, were on the left. Cornwallis could not bring himself to surrender in person and his sword was delivered by General Charles O'Hara, his second-in-command, to General Lincoln,

Henry Clinton "had the faculty of . . . never working in harmony with his principal subordinate officer," Lord Cornwallis. Short and paunchy, extremely cautious, suspicious of those around him, and too timid to make fast decisions, he tried after the war to shift to Cornwallis all blame for defeat.

General Cornwallis had opposed colonial taxation, a courageous stand which forced him to withdraw from the House of Lords. But his loyalty was unquestioned by King George, who raised his rank and sent him off to fight in America, despite Lady Cornwallis' entreaties that he be kept at home.

Washington's deputy. With great reluctance the British officers ordered their troops to ground arms. One New Jersey officer reported that they "behaved like boys who had been whipped at school. Some bit their lips; some pouted; others cried." The soldiers sullenly threw their arms on the ground in heaps. Then they returned to their encampment, guarded by the Allied forces.

There is a tradition—one which can be neither proved nor disproved—that when the British and Hessian troops marched out to surrender, a British band played "The World Turned Upside Down." Certainly no song title could have been more appropriate to the occasion. Yorktown, for the British, was truly a "world turned upside down." According to an eyewitness, Lord North took the news "as he would have taken a ball in his breast." "Oh God! it is all over!" he repeated many times. When George III acknowledged receipt of the bad news by letter, he failed to note the hour and the minute of his writing, which had been his unfailing habit.

Peace was now inevitable, but not necessarily British recognition of American independence. George III, along with a substantial portion of the British ruling class, hated to abandon all sovereignty over the Thirteen Colonies. Long before Yorktown the British had tried to bring the American war to an end, but always with a formula short of independence. Such an offer might have tempted Congress had Britain, before the adoption of the Declaration of Independence, offered as much as it was willing to concede after Saratoga; at least, a large segment of American opinion might have been won over. Again and again, however, it had been the story of too little, too late.

By 1780 both sides seemed anxious to devise a formula for ending the war. The solution appeared to be foreign mediation. The British would have preferred Austrian intervention; France, on the other hand, wanted Russian mediation, counting on more sympathy for the Allied cause in St. Petersburg than in Vienna. Late in 1780, Austria and Russia agreed upon a joint mediation effort in Vienna. But nothing came of it, because England was reluctant to recognize the independence of the Thirteen Colonies. Austria and Russia had a plan to force a truce and impose a settlement based on the military status quo. If they had succeeded, Maine, New York City, and most of the Carolinas and Georgia would have remained part of the British Empire, and a united nation might never have been achieved. The truth was that the countries named as mediators had no interest whatsoever in American independence and would have settled for a great deal less.

The news of Yorktown put an end to this complicated diplomatic minuet and smashed all prospects of outside mediation. In England the mood hardened for quick peace. On March 4, 1782, the House of Commons passed a resolution to consider as enemies of the king and country all those who should further attempt to carry on the war. Two weeks later Lord North's ministry resigned. George III went so far as to prepare a draft of his own abdication. Lord Rockingham, a good friend of America, headed the new government. His foreign secretary was Charles James Fox, a longtime advocate of American independence. The road seemed cleared for quick recognition of the new nation, but the crucial post of secretary of colonial affairs went to the Earl of Shelburne, who held fast to two contradictory positions: he was opposed both to prolonging the war and to granting independence.

When Parliament authorized the administration to make a peace or truce

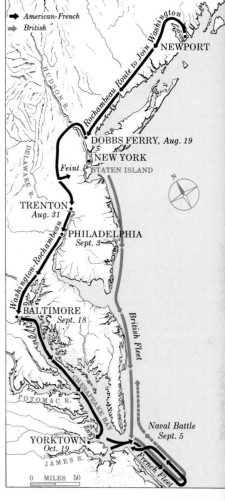

THE TRAP AT YORKTOWN:

AUTUMN, 1781

Seizing a splendid opportunity, Washington determined to march from New York to Yorktown (black line) and trap the British. Joined at Dobbs Ferry by Rochambeau's French troops, he crossed the Hudson to Stony Point, feinted at General Clinton, then sped south. The British, suddenly aware of his bold plan, rushed their own fleet south (brown line), but they were forced to withdraw after a battle with the French off Virginia. De Grasse then sailed up the Chesapeake to Baltimore and ferried the Allied armies to Yorktown to begin the siege that ended the Revolution.

with America, a fierce rivalry broke out between Fox and Shelburne to dominate the negotiations. Shelburne claimed that since the independence of the 13 states was not yet conceded, they were still colonies. Therefore negotiations with them came under his jurisdiction, while Fox could settle with France and Spain. Accordingly, Shelburne dispatched Richard Oswald, a pro-American merchant and slave trader, to France to start preliminary talks with Franklin, while Fox sent Thomas Grenville to do the same with Count de Vergennes, the French foreign minister. This divided authority did not last long; on July 1 Rockingham died. Fox quit as foreign secretary, and Shelburne became prime minister, still dreaming of a reconciliation based on American autonomy short of complete independence.

THE fate of America rested in the hands of the ablest delegation the United States has ever sent to a conference table. The three American peace commissioners were Benjamin Franklin, who had been in France throughout the war; John Jay, who reached Paris from Spain at the end of June; and John Adams, who arrived from Holland in October after successfully negotiating a substantial loan from the Dutch. A fourth commissioner, Henry Laurens, had previously been captured by the British and confined in the Tower of London. He was ultimately released, but he was not able to make his way to Paris until negotiations were almost completed.

The American commissioners held out against the British, their French allies and in fact the world for what they considered irreducible terms. Congress had instructed the commissioners to abide by the advice of the French government. But Vergennes was willing to allow the Americans to confer separately, so long as he was consulted and a joint peace made at the end.

Franklin began the talks. When he became indisposed, John Jay took over. Jay's frigid reception at the Spanish court had made him suspicious of, if not hostile to, the aims and ethics of European diplomacy. He refused to carry on peace talks with the British until independence itself was conceded, fearing not only British trickery but a Franco-Spanish betrayal. His liveliest apprehensions were aroused when he learned that Vergennes' under secretary, Joseph Rayneval, had made a secret trip to London. His purpose was to sound out Shelburne on peace terms between England and Spain, but Jay feared Rayneval would propose dividing the trans-Appalachian territory among England, the United States and Spain, a settlement Rayneval was known to favor. Jay now decided to push separate negotiations with England. Justifying this disregard of instructions to act with the advice of France, John Adams wrote Robert R. Livingston, America's foreign secretary, that "America has . . . been a football between contending nations from the beginning, and it is easy to foresee that France and England both will endeavor to involve us in their future wars." Jay put it more strongly: "we have no rational dependence except on God and ourselves."

Shelburne at last realized that the 13 states would settle for nothing less than independence. With Jay willing, if not anxious, to make a separate peace, Shelburne met the Americans most of the way by empowering the British delegation to deal with "the Commissioners of the United States of America." Jay accepted this formula, and the talks moved ahead. Although Franklin had originally demanded Canada (listing it as an "advisable" though not a "necessary" condition), Jay now dropped this demand for fear that France and Spain

George Washington drubs Britannia while Holland, France and Spain look on in this 1783 British cartoon. Washington's feminine attire was probably inspired by rumors that Martha Washington had said on her deathbed that her husband was a woman. Actually, Martha was still very much alive.

would block America's claim to the Mississippi River, to which the British had offered no objection.

On September 30, 1782, news reached England of the failure of a Franco-Spanish attack on Gibraltar. The British stiffened, and the Americans had to make a few concessions they might not have had to grant earlier. They agreed to recognize the validity of prewar debts owed to British creditors, and they promised that Congress would recommend that the states repeal those acts confiscating the estates of British subjects. Both of these were to create vexing issues in the years ahead.

But the enormous gains of the Americans at the conference table far outweighed their concessions. Independence was assured. A great territory extending to the Mississippi was won. After a hard battle, John Adams was able to confirm America's right to fish off Canada, despite backstage French opposition. "Thanks be to God," Adams wrote, "that our Tom Cod are safe in spite of the malice of enemies, the finesse of allies, and the mistakes of Congress." Finally, the treaty contained a separate secret article to the effect that in case West Florida should be British at the end of the war, its boundary should be somewhat farther north than if it were to remain in the hands of Spain. Since Spain kept the Floridas, which she had reconquered during the war, this article never went into effect.

Franklin prudently omitted including the secret article when he sent Vergennes a copy of the preliminary treaty which the American commissioners had already signed with England. Vergennes was annoyed by what he regarded as the precipitate action of the Americans in signing the preliminary articles before consulting him, and flabbergasted by Britain's generosity to her rebellious subjects. As a professional diplomat, the count bitingly remarked: "The English buy peace rather than make it." But Franklin's superb tact prevented an open breach between the Allies.

On September 3, 1783, the American and British negotiators signed the final peace in a little hotel on the Rue Jacob in Paris. The same day, France and Spain signed the peace with England at Versailles and, in a courteous gesture to the would-be mediators, also authorized the Austrian and Russian plenipotentiaries to sign. Summing up, Benjamin Franklin observed, "there never was a good war or a bad peace."

A WORLD war had ended. From the first successful revolution of modern times of colonies against a mother country, a new nation had emerged. Tom Paine exulted in a closing "Crisis" paper written April 19, 1783: " 'The times that tried men's souls' are over—and the greatest and completest revolution the world ever knew, gloriously and happily accomplished."

"With our fate," Washington predicted, "will the destiny of unborn millions be involved." European observers were less sanguine about the success of the experiment in independence. There was a basis for their doubt. The victory won in war may have seemed to be a complete solution to American problems. Actually, all that victory had accomplished was to shift the responsibility for the future of America from absentee rulers in London to freely chosen representatives of the new nation. Though America had attained freedom, it had no guarantee of survival, which could be achieved only through national unity. The critical months and years ahead would determine whether the new confederation could create this indispensable national unity.

Illumination.

COLONEL TILGHMAN, Aid de Camp to his Excellency General WASHINGTON, having brought official acounts of the SURRENDER of Lord Cornwallis, and the Garrisons of York and Gloucester, those Citizens who chuse to ILLUMINATE on the GLORIOUS OCCASION, will do it this evening at Six, and extinguish their lights at Nine o'clock.

Decorum and harmony are earnestly recommended to every Citizen, and a general discountenance to the least appearance of riot.

October 24, 1781.

A triumphant Philadelphia handbill announces the victory at Yorktown. The news, which arrived three days after Cornwallis' surrender, was tempered with a warning. The city's Committee of Safety advised calmness amidst the cannon fire, rockets and bonfires that signaled the end of the fighting.

George III was depicted in silhouette by his daughter Elizabeth, nicknamed "The Muse" for her artistic talent. She published several volumes of drawings, the first when she was 25. In order to help care for her aging father, she remained single until she was 48, two years before the king's death.

CREATOR of U.S. naval tradition, John Paul Jones is seen as a pirate in British caricature. This was a backhanded tribute to daring and effective raids in Britain's home waters. Most feared of all the Revolutionary naval leaders, this Scottish gardener's son was denounced by the English as a renegade murderer.

The sea war: slow, arduous triumph

UNTIL nearly the end of the Revolution, overwhelming naval superiority gave the British an immense advantage in the war. The colonists, with a wilderness at their backs and overland travel between their seaport cities primitive at best, were largely dependent on shipping. Free access to the sea was vital to their foreign trade, whaling and fisheries, as well as to most of their domestic commerce and communication. The population was strung out along a thousand miles of eastern seaboard, and the British, from the ports they captured, could disrupt American supply lines on land as well as at sea. So royal troops struck wherever they chose while the Patriots had to slog after them in exhausting marches. The American Navy was born in glorious travail. American seamen in American ships, always outnumbered and outgunned, fought valiantly throughout the war, constantly harassing the British fleet and capturing quantities of valuable supplies. And in the end, a French fleet supplied the decisive maritime superiority which Washington so desperately needed by sealing off Yorktown and keeping supplies from besieged Cornwallis. Thus, to the early accomplishments of U.S. naval heroes was also added a fraternal bond with France which has never been forgotten.

THE FIERCEST FIGHT of the war at sea is memorialized here. In the epic 1779 battle between *Bonhomme Richard*, Jones's flagship *(left)*, and Britain's *Serapis*, a British convoy was the prize.

The two ships fought all day. Jones's refusal to surrender—"I have not yet begun to fight!"—made him famous. Finally, by moonlight, the battered and broken *Serapis* struck her colors.

British frigates "Phoenix" and "Rose" underscore the colonies' helplessness by calmly passing between Forts Washington and Lee in 1776.

The troubled growth of an infant navy

THE birth date of the Continental navy is generally accepted as October 30, 1775, when the Continental Congress appointed a Naval Committee and authorized the creation of a fighting force. The situation throughout most of the war is more accurately reflected in the painting above. In 1776, a little more than a year after the decision to found the navy, three British frigates could cruise unscathed up the Hudson past New York, ignoring the fire from two American forts. The range of these cannon was much too short, and no patriot ship could stop this calm demonstration of British superiority.

The Revolutionary navy never was able to reach the wartime strength its planners may have hoped for. In all, 13 frigates were built (the rest of the fleet, some 40 ships, were converted merchantmen). Many of these were manned by resourceful men, and some achieved glory even in adversity. The *Randolph*, off Barbados in 1778, effectively challenged a British ship twice her size and fought valiantly until a shot exploded her powder magazine *(left)*, killing 300 men.

Some individual colonies had navies too, primarily for local defense. The strongest American force at sea remained some 2,000 privately owned men-of-war that captured 600 British ships and $18 million in supplies.

JOHN PAUL JONES ESEK HOPKINS

JOHN BARRY JOSHUA BARNEY

END OF THE "RANDOLPH" shows the American frigate, commanded by Captain Nicholas Biddle, torn by a fearful explosion *(left)* after a battle with Britain's *Yarmouth*.

GALLERY OF CAPTAINS reflects the varied nature of the infant navy. John Paul Jones is its most heroic symbol; Esek Hopkins, commander-in-chief of the fleet, was sacked as incompetent; Irish-born John Barry was a far-ranging raider; Joshua Barney, thrice captured, survived to fight in the War of 1812.

A fleet defeated from shore

Weak as the colonies were at sea, it is not surprising that their first victory over a British fleet was won on land. It was a notable triumph, not only militarily, but also because it showed that the southern colonies held firm to the cause of liberty. Britain had had reason to doubt this. So in the spring of 1776 a pow-

erful fleet of warships, commanded by Commodore Sir Peter Parker, joined a force of 2,500 sea-borne troops under General Sir Henry Clinton to attack Charleston and win it for the British cause. During the close-in attack on June 28, the patriots fought back doggedly from Fort Sullivan in the harbor. Earth-works and barricades of palmetto logs, seen above in the painting done in 1815 by John Blake White, absorbed 7,000 British cannon balls while Colonel William Moultrie's men coolly decimated both the invaders and the fleet. Commodore Parker, his breeches torn by a shell splinter, sailed north to find safety.

95

A hard life at sea, a living death in prison ships

AN INFAMOUS HULK, the British prison ship *Jersey* lies at anchor off Brooklyn. This floating concentration camp was the most notorious of a group of these noisome vessels. Once a proud ship of the line, she was filled with agony and disease, a ship that meant death for some 11,000 American prisoners.

A SEAMAN'S life on an 18th Century warship, with its cramped quarters *(below)*, bad food and brutal punishment, was hard even in peace. In war, and especially a far-flung war like the American Revolution, it was at times unbearable. Between 1774 and 1780, the British navy lost some 60,000 men by desertion and death.

For many of those aboard the British warships, the term of service began with their forcible conscription. Others were lured to a tavern and when they were dead drunk, the "King's shilling," symbol of voluntary enlistment, was pressed into their hands. Once in the service, discipline was merciless. Desertion was punishable by death, the least infraction by flogging; six dozen lashes were not uncommon.

The navy itself, under the dissipated Earl of Sandwich, was riddled with corruption. Graft was widespread, new ships were jerry-built, dockyards and repairs neglected. One old ship of the line, the *Royal George*, literally fell apart at Spithead in 1782 and sank with some 800 seamen and visitors aboard. Ship supplies were sold for politicians' profit, and even the normally sparse rations were frequently short or spoiled.

Worst of all, however, was the lot of the Americans who fell into British hands after battles at sea. To the British, the Americans were all guilty of rebellion, and privateers were considered no more than pirates. The only reprieve offered prisoners was service in the British navy. Some accepted; most did not, and the dreadful prison ships became their jail and often their grave.

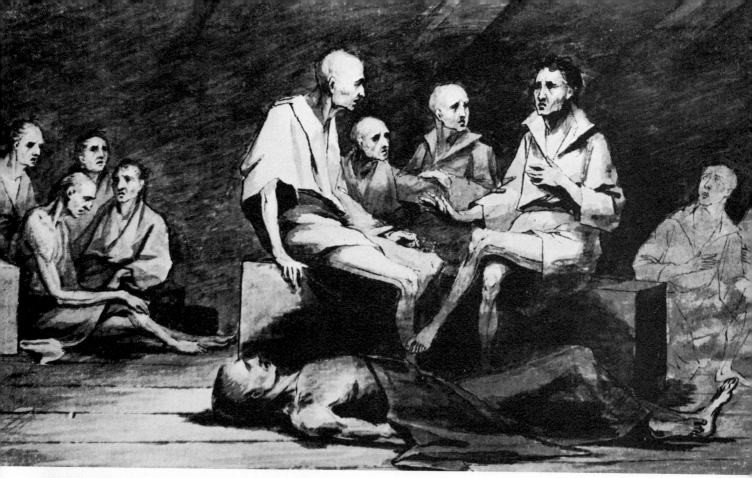

WRETCHEDNESS on board the *Jersey* is eloquently portrayed *(above)* by John Trumbull in his contemporary sketch. Suffocating in heat of summer, freezing in winter, hapless starving prisoners had only a small chance to survive the "nauseous and putrid atmosphere." Many soldiers preferred death to capture.

THE CROWDED HARDSHIP of the sailors' life is shown in this cutaway drawing *(below)* of a typical frigate with its two gun decks. Officers had relatively spacious quarters aft, but crews, confined in the bows, were ill fed and worse housed. Culprits in brig *(center)* were at waterline, horses were stowed below that.

The British (right) mulishly maintain formation off Yorktown in this inaccurate painting by Théodore Gudin. Meanwhile, the French

HAND-TO-HAND SEA FIGHT like the one shown above is more typical of Americans in their adventurous hit-and-run naval warfare than of the formal maneuvers of British and French fleets.

This picture by Ferdinand Perrot, who could be as inaccurate as his master Théodore Gudin (the British flag at right was not used until 1813), was painted long after the Revolution ended.

fleet launches the key battle which doomed Cornwallis. Neither side lost a vessel in this strange sea fight that ended in virtual stalemate.

A fleet to the rescue, a cork in the bottle

THE painting above, as dramatic as it is imaginative, for the two fleets were actually on almost parallel courses, depicts the fateful moment which finally gave Washington control of the sea. Fought far from land in September 1781, this engagement sealed the fate of the British as a cork seals the contents in a bottle. The bottle was made up of French troops under Lafayette and Rochambeau, and the Americans under Washington. The American commander, learning that Admiral de Grasse had sailed from the West Indies to come to his aid, swiftly diverted his forces from New York and led them in a magnificent forced march to Yorktown. There Cornwallis, relying on British sea power, had based his army. In a five-day, standoff battle marked by the disastrous adherence of Admiral Thomas Graves to the Royal Navy's outmoded *Fighting Instructions*, De Grasse outmaneuvered the British. Badly mauled, Graves had to concede "the impracticability of giving any effectual succour to General Earl Cornwallis" and withdraw to New York. His escape route plugged off, Cornwallis had to surrender.

DE GRASSE, ". . . six feet tall most days, six feet six on days of battle," is famed for the victory called the "one decisive engagement of the war."

GRAVES is recalled as the English admiral who rigidly followed the traditional rules when initiative and innovation might have won the day.

99

A hush at Yorktown

While Admiral de Grasse hovered off Yorktown, the Franco-American army was pressing hard on the suddenly desperate Cornwallis. With escape by sea impossible, he had one slim hope left: to get over the York River to Gloucester Point and drive north. But a violent autumn squall blew up and cut

that off too, and now the American and French guns began to rumble and roar. On October 17, 1781, smoke hung thick over Yorktown, but at 10 a.m. a sudden hush set in. A white cloth appeared on the British ramparts. Cornwallis was asking for terms. Two days later the surrender was signed, and past the quiet ranks of the Revolutionary allies *(above)* an entire British army marched to stack its arms and turn over its 7,241 men, some 7,000 muskets, 200 cannon, 450 horses, 25 transports, quantities of supplies and $11,000 in cash. It would be nearly two years before the peace was signed, but the war was over.

5. THE CRISIS
OF FREEDOM

THE morning of November 25, 1783, began brisk and clear in New York City. As redcoats were rowed out to the British fleet waiting in the harbor, American troops entered the city, followed by caravans of patriots returning to their homes. To the sounds of cheering crowds and booming guns, the Stars and Stripes was hoisted.

But as the returning residents looked about, they saw little reason for cheers. The city they had known in 1776 had deteriorated badly during the war. At least a quarter of New York, twice gutted by fires, was in utter ruin. The rest looked shabby and neglected. Once-handsome dwellings still bore the wounds of military occupation and some had been stripped by the hastily departing Tories. Streets and pavements were torn up, lamps were shattered, rubbish lay everywhere. What was true of New York was equally true of New London, Fairfield, Norfolk and Charleston; of the wracked and pillaged countryside of the Mohawk Valley and the Jerseys, the cockpits of the war; of devastated Virginia and the lower South. The American Confederation confronted a huge task of reconstruction.

However, the Confederation's principal difficulty was a political one. This was the problem of building loyalty to the new nation. The Revolutionary veteran Samuel Shaw, soon to be the first United States consul in China, declared in 1783, "We are thirteen states, and *a hoop to the barrel* is the prevailing sentiment." But Shaw was exaggerating the national desire for cohesion.

A DEDICATED FEDERALIST, Alexander Hamilton is remembered for urging a strong central government. He called the Confederation "fit neither for war nor peace."

There was a strong feeling of separatism pervading the 13 states, and in a way the success of the Revolution had bolstered this feeling. For many patriots had been fighting to restore the local autonomy they had once enjoyed under the rule of the crown.

Many of the leaders of the Revolution were profoundly concerned about their ability to create a sense of loyalty to the new nation, to reconcile national patriotism with long-existing attachment to native states. They wondered whether they could get provincial-minded people to "think continentally," as Alexander Hamilton put it. Hamilton especially hammered away at the theme of molding and preserving "a national character," of giving the Confederation effective powers. ". . . the republic is sick and wants powerful remedies," he had written in 1781, when he was already prepared with a detailed blueprint for the future. He feared "a number of petty states, with the appearance only of union, jarring, jealous and perverse, without any determined direction, fluctuating and unhappy at home, weak and insignificant by their dissensions in the eyes of other nations." In 1782 he had confessed, "The more I see, the more I find reason for those who love this country to weep over its blindness." "We are placed among the nations of the earth," Washington concluded to Lafayette in 1783, "and have a character to establish, but how we shall acquit ourselves time must discover."

Churchman Josiah Tucker, one of many Britons who predicted failure for the Confederation, never did believe the American experiment would work. At the time of the Revolution, he urged Britain to free the colonies because he was sure that they would soon get into trouble and beg to be taken back.

EUROPEANS, in general, felt even less optimism about America's prospects. The astute political economist, Josiah Tucker, Dean of England's Gloucester Cathedral, pronounced "the future grandeur of America one of the idlest and most visionary notions that ever was conceived even by writers of romance." According to Tucker, the Americans' clashing interests, and differences of governments and manners, left them with "no center of union and no common interest. . . . A disunited people till the end of time, suspicious and distrustful of each other, they will be divided and subdivided into little commonwealths or principalities, according to natural boundaries." Count de Vergennes, France's foreign minister, and in many respects the European best informed on American affairs, observed in 1784, "the American Confederation has a great tendency toward dissolution."

The one unifying element was the Congress of the Confederation, but its power was so shaky that it offered a feeble foundation on which to build. By 1783 its prestige was so low that some states no longer bothered to send representatives. Even the presidency of Congress, nominally the highest office in America, was treated with little respect. John Hancock, who was elected to that office in 1785, never even came to New York, where Congress held its sessions. James Sullivan, a prominent Massachusetts lawyer, once urged an infirm friend to accept the post, calling it "the Easiest in the Union for an invalid." After dining with President Cyrus Griffin and several members of Congress in 1788, John Adams' daughter wrote her mother, "Had you been present you would have trembled for your country, to have seen, heard and observed the men who are its rulers."

John Jay won great respect for his skill as a diplomat in behalf of the American cause. After he helped negotiate the 1783 Treaty of Paris with Great Britain, his fellow negotiator John Adams wrote of him in admiration, "Mr. Jay returns to his country like a bee to his hive, loaded with meat and honor."

With all its weaknesses, Congress managed to ratify the peace, establish executive departments and administer the western territories. Considering the handicaps under which it operated, these were remarkable feats, counterbalanced however by the fact that so many eminent men of affairs had left the national scene. Washington was back home at his beloved Mount Vernon.

Jefferson had been sent to Paris, John Adams to London. Hamilton and young James Madison were in their home states: the former practicing law in New York; the latter active in the Virginia House of Delegates, where he was largely responsible for a thorough revision of the laws and for the adoption of Jefferson's Statute for Religious Freedom. A disillusioned Robert Morris, despairing of cooperation between Congress and the states, resigned the post of Superintendent of Finance in 1784 to concentrate on his private business affairs. Robert R. Livingston quit as Secretary for Foreign Affairs for the more lucrative chancellorship of New York. Patrick Henry, John Hancock and George Clinton preferred to serve as governors of their respective states, Benjamin Franklin as president of Pennsylvania's Executive Council.

There was one towering figure who continued to be active in the affairs of the Confederation, the new Secretary for Foreign Affairs, John Jay. His reputation as a negotiator had been enhanced by his diplomatic experience in Madrid and Paris, and the three years abroad had taught him a great deal about the devious ways of foreign chancelleries. No man seemed better qualified to put America's relations with other nations on a sound and peaceful footing than this tall, lean man of conscience from New York.

Jay stanchly advocated strengthening the central government and giving its administrators more responsibility. He saw to it that all communications on foreign affairs were made through his department rather than through Congress. He had only two clerks and a two-room suite, but from his cramped quarters there radiated a growing power. The French minister to the United States grudgingly reported in 1786: "The political importance of Mr. Jay increases daily. Congress seems to me to be guided only by his directions, and it is as difficult to obtain anything without the cooperation of that minister as to bring about the rejection of a measure proposed by him."

Jay was keenly aware that his government's authority at home could never be secure until its independence was unquestioned abroad. But it proved an easier task to pursue an independent course than to win the respect of the great powers. Jay's troubles in getting the provisions of the peace treaty with England carried out demonstrated how difficult it was for America to gain international stature.

THE grudging steps by which England recognized America's independence had served notice that the mother country was unlikely to fulfill its treaty obligations with speed or enthusiasm. Franklin had talked of "sweet reconciliation," and the American peace commissioners at Paris had shown that they were eager to resume trade with Britain on terms of full reciprocity. If Lord Shelburne had remained at the helm, Britain might, just possibly, have granted its former colonies their prewar commercial privileges. But his ministry was toppled and, as England realized that it had little to fear from American trade reprisals under the Confederation, pressure developed to keep the Americans from trading with the British sugar islands, and an Order in Council to that effect was issued on July 2, 1783.

When William Pitt the Younger became prime minister, he bowed to the views of businessmen who regarded mercantilism and the Navigation Acts as the prime safeguard of English prosperity. One of their spokesmen, Lord Sheffield, marshaled statistics to prove that American trade had nowhere to go except Britain and argued that Congress was impotent to retaliate, no

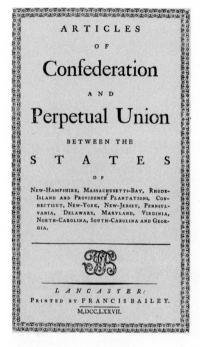

This official copy of the Articles of Confederation was published in Lancaster, Pennsylvania, where Congress met in 1777. Though the Confederation endured only eight years, the title page hopefully predicted "perpetual union," and one newspaper exulted that the nation had "been indissolubly cemented."

matter how distasteful subservience to England might be. "It will not be an easy matter," he asserted, "to bring the American States to act as a nation; they are not to be feared as such by us." Convinced, indeed, that the United States was about to fall apart, Britain sacrificed long-range friendship for short-term profits. John Adams, America's first minister to England, was coolly treated. The British did not trouble to send a minister to America. Until Congress could regulate commerce and impose tariff prohibitions, Jay was powerless to extort a trade treaty from England.

Still more ominous to the new nation's security was Britain's refusal to withdraw troops from the frontier posts on American soil. As Jay saw it, Britain held them "as pledges of enmity," and used them to stir up Indian unrest. To preserve peace, Jay advised Congress, America must be prepared for war. But America, which had abruptly disbanded its army, was not equipped to fight a full-scale war with a great power, or even, for that matter, able to pacify Indians.

Jay conceded that Britain had some justification for its arrogant course, for America was flagrantly ignoring two provisions of the peace treaty. One state after another had put obstacles in the way of British creditors trying to collect prewar debts. The Virginia debtors were the largest single group that owed money to Britain, and their spokesman, Patrick Henry, got the Virginia Assembly to defeat an attempted repeal of laws nullifying the debts. Although Virginia finally did pass a bill that validated English claims, it had a provision that kept it from going into effect until Britain evacuated the frontier posts and paid for the slaves taken from patriot planters during the war. The fact is that few of the Virginia debtors had either the means or the inclination to fulfill the debt provisions of the peace treaty. In the end, it was neither state legislatures nor federal courts that secured payment of the debts. Under the settlement agreed on by the Jay Treaty of 1794, the national government took over most of the burdens of the private debtors.

THERE was another provocation to England: the continued confiscation by the states of Tory property in violation of the peace treaty. Indeed, the confiscations had been stepped up sharply after the war was over. Nationalists who felt that America's good name required observance of the treaty thought this vindictive. But the Confederation, which had been unable to prevent Tories from being lynched in the South or tarred and feathered in New Jersey, was poorly equipped to compel the states to honor the unpopular provisions of the peace treaty.

The confiscation issue was soon tested in New York. In 1783 the state legislature passed an act enabling those who had fled from the enemy to sue for damage done to their property during their absence; defendants could not justify damage by citing any military order or enemy command. Soon after this act was passed, Elizabeth Rutgers sued a wealthy Tory merchant named Waddington, who had operated her brewery under British military orders after she had fled New York City in 1776. Alexander Hamilton defended the Tory, at considerable peril to his popularity, and won the case. The court refused damages for the period when the brewery was used "for the carrying on of the war," in effect annulling the statute as contrary to the treaty (and also anticipating the doctrine of judicial review). Both Hamilton and the court were denounced for upholding the treaty, but Washington supported them,

Simon Kenton spent an adventurous life in the West. Rising from a daring 19-year-old scout to become a brigadier general of militia, he fought the British and Indians for 40 tumultuous years. He was captured twice by Indians, and twice escaped. Perhaps his chief claim to fame is that he once saved the life of that other and better-known American folk hero, Daniel Boone.

asserting that "reason seems very much in favor of the opinion of the court, and my judgment yields a hearty assent to it."

But the spirit of moderation spread slowly. Most of the confiscations were permanent, and Congress and Britain had to shoulder the burden of compensating Loyalists for their losses. It took time to heal the wounds, but by 1786 John Jay could write Shelburne, then Lord Lansdowne, that Tories who had previously been disqualified were again sitting in state legislatures and had been restored to the practice of the law.

JAY'S two years in Madrid had prepared him for the long, stubborn postwar negotiations with Spain. The thorniest issue was America's insistence on free navigation of the Mississippi to the sea. Spain, opposed to America's claims beyond the Appalachians throughout the peace negotiations, officially closed the lower Mississippi to citizens of the new nation and levied taxes and tariffs at New Orleans on American products coming down the river. This was a grave blow to the Western settlers for whom it was much easier to ship farm produce to the East via the Mississippi than by land across the rugged Appalachians. Western settlers had increased rapidly after the war; there were 50,000 in Kentucky and Tennessee alone by 1785 (see page 114). As population grew, demands for free use of the river became more strident.

In 1785 Spain dispatched Don Diego de Gardoqui to negotiate a settlement of the outstanding issues with America. He had been instructed to keep exclusive control of the Mississippi for Spain at any cost. Gardoqui spoke English well, had the advantage of a previous acquaintance with Jay in Madrid, and enjoyed a generous expense account, which enabled him to rent a fine mansion in New York City and to entertain public figures. He offered America a liberal trade treaty, but was adamant on the Mississippi. As the negotiations dragged on, Jay began to fear a joint move by Spain and Britain to sever the West from the Union, and he was persuaded that it might be prudent for the United States to "forbear" using the Mississippi during the life of the proposed treaty. Jay was convinced that the Mississippi would almost certainly come under American control one day and he, like Washington, considered "forbearance" to be only a stopgap arrangement. But opposition from southern states prevented the two thirds majority in Congress needed to ratify a treaty. Easterners supported "forbearance," though for a selfish reason: a treaty would discourage immigration to the West, which cheapened the value of the backlands in eastern states by drawing labor into the interior, and would offer substantial trade advantages as well. Jay finally told Congress that the alternatives were to make a treaty or go to war. "A treaty disagreeable to one half of the nation had better not be made, for it would be violated," he noted, while "a war disliked by the other half, would promise but little success, especially under a government so greatly affected by public opinion." Prepared neither to go to war nor to digest so unpalatable a concession, Congress deferred the question for consideration by the new federal government.

Even France, America's wartime ally, scarcely bothered to veil her contempt for the Confederation. In a thoughtless moment, the aging Franklin had signed a consular agreement under which the "Thirteen United States of North America" permitted French consuls to present their commissions to the governors of the states in which they would reside, rather than to Congress. The arrangement was insulting to national sovereignty, as was another

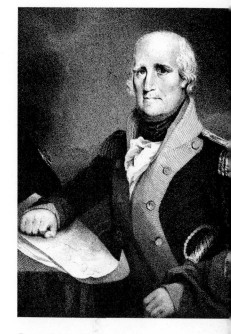

George Rogers Clark, who helped fix America's claim to the West, was a gifted amateur archeologist. Speculating on strange mounds found in the western valleys, he suggested that they were built by ancient Indians, a theory modern science confirmed. George's brother William was co-commander of the 1804-1806 Lewis and Clark expedition that explored the Far West.

provision of the treaty that allowed France to curb emigration of her subjects to America and to block their becoming naturalized American citizens.

Although the agreement was eventually renegotiated by Jefferson, and its more offensive features were eliminated, the original provisions had betrayed France's desire for a weak America. The French looked upon America as a protégé and their diplomatic representatives tended to behave more like stern guardians than like ministers to a sovereign state. The vain and arrogant behavior was the reason why Jay requested the recall of the French minister, Count de Moustier—although Moustier's rumored affair with his own sister-in-law may have hastened the envoy's downfall.

While the conduct of the European powers posed threats to the prestige of the young nation, the enslavement of America's mariners by the Barbary States revealed the impotence of the Confederation. Before the Revolution no colonial ships could sail the Mediterranean without the protection of the British fleet. With independence Americans lost this protection. For $30,000 worth of gifts, an American emissary, Thomas Barclay, purchased from Morocco permission for Yankee ships to sail unmolested in the Mediterranean. But Algiers, Tunis and Tripoli set much higher prices, demanding several million dollars in all. These were staggering sums for a Congress too poor either to buy off the pirates or to build the navy needed to smash them. Weighing the various humiliations visited on America, John Jay thought that they might have a salutary effect in the long run. "The more we are ill-treated abroad," he observed, "the more we shall unite and consolidate at home."

IT was clear that the solution to certain problems could be achieved only through united action by the states. A conspicuous example was the settlement of the conflicting claims of the original states to the western lands beyond the Appalachian Mountains. Massachusetts, Connecticut, New York, Virginia, the Carolinas and Georgia all asserted such claims, on the basis either of colonial charters or of Indian treaties. As far back as 1754 Franklin had proposed, in his Albany plan, that the western domain be turned over to a central authority. In 1777 Maryland revived the idea that the western lands should be regarded as America's common possession and refused to ratify the Articles of Confederation until New York and Virginia had given up their extravagant claims. As one Maryland delegate to Congress declared: "No colony has a right to go to the South Sea; they never had; they can't have. It would not be safe to the rest." To placate Maryland, Congress urged in 1780 that all the claimant states cede their lands to the national government, which would eventually form them into separate states, to be admitted to the union on terms of equality with the original 13. This farsighted proposal, foreshadowing the later Northwest Ordinance, was not acted on immediately, but eventually all the states yielded their claims.

The continued assertion of claims to the western lands resulted in small-scale shooting wars and conspiratorial plots. Pennsylvania and Virginia fought in the Pittsburgh region before finally agreeing to respect a westward extension of the Mason and Dixon Line as their boundary. Pennsylvanians used arms to oust Connecticut settlers who claimed the Wyoming Valley under their state's old charter. Land speculators and settlers threatened to force the secession of Kentucky from Virginia and of Tennessee from North Carolina. James Wilkinson, whose conduct as an officer during the Revolution had left

An idealized Indian maiden symbolized America being reconciled with the mother country, Britannia, in this optimistic English cartoon, published during the 1782 peace talks. Before the figure of Uncle Sam became the U.S. symbol, cartoonists also pictured America as a rattlesnake, an eagle and a bucking horse. This tobacco-clad girl evolved into today's Columbia.

him with a shady reputation, schemed endlessly to separate Kentucky from Virginia and then to join it to Spain, for which he was secretly working. Settlers in the Tennessee area organized the short-lived "free state of Franklin," electing John Sevier governor.

Even during the Revolution, Ethan Allen and his brother Ira attempted to negotiate a treaty with Britain which would have made Vermont a province of Canada. While the real objective of the Allens may have been to force Congress to side with the Green Mountain Boys against New York, which claimed the territory, talk of making Vermont a British province continued in the Confederation period. All these secessionist threats had to await solution until the federal government was established, after which Vermont, Kentucky and Tennessee were promptly admitted to the Union.

The Northwest Ordinance, greatest achievement of the Congress of the Confederation, was adopted in July 1787, at the very moment that the Constitutional Convention, meeting in Philadelphia, was drafting a far-reaching plan to replace the Confederation itself. The ordinance provided for three stages of government in the new lands north of the Ohio River. First, they would be administered by a governor, a secretary and three judges named by Congress. As soon as there were 5,000 free adult males in the territory, authority would reside in an elected legislature. Finally, when the population reached 60,000 in any given area, that section could become a state and be entirely equal with the existing states. Not more than five states could be carved out of the territory. (Eventually these became Ohio, Indiana, Illinois, Michigan and Wisconsin.) The Northwest Ordinance was also notable for its guarantees of freedom of worship, civil liberties and public support of education. Moreover, it showed foresight in prohibiting slavery. Above all, it set a significant precedent for the handling of American territories, not as colonies, but as entities moving toward statehood and equality.

Congress was not nearly so successful when it turned to several other issues threatening to blow the new nation apart. Divisive sectionalism seemed to be in the ascendant everywhere, and its persistent strength during the years of the Confederation persuaded many sober statesmen that the United States was simply too large to remain united. General Benjamin Lincoln thought that peace and safety might best be secured by "a firm alliance between the divisions" rather than by union. New Englanders like Theodore Sedgwick favored setting up a "northern confederation," and Jefferson spoke of the difficulties between the sections. "God bless them both," he said of East and West, "and keep them in union, if it be for their good, but separate them, if it be better." There were serious divisions even within the older states; in several of them, back-country citizens demanded a larger voice as population pressed westward, forcing a shift in state capitals from the coast to the interior.

FINANCE was another area in which the Confederation proved impotent to manage the problems thrust upon it. Congress started its postwar operations with a debt of almost $40 million, not including the debts of the several states. But the government had no dependable sources of revenues. The old system of requisitions on the states had largely broken down. At the close of 1783, less than 15 per cent of the $10 million requested had been paid by the states. At one point Robert Morris declared that talking to the states about money was like preaching to the dead. Congress plumbed the depths of

A realistic American Indian, this scalp-waving brave appeared in an English volume of 1789. The author, a British war veteran, told of how General Burgoyne had encouraged Indian allies to "take the scalps of the dead, when killed by your fire and in fair opposition" but warned (in vain) that "on no account . . . are they to be taken from the wounded or even dying."

financial degradation in 1783, when it authorized Morris to draw on the credit of loans from foreign governments while our envoys were still negotiating for them. Fortunately, Dutch bankers came to the rescue with substantial advances that tided Congress over for a time.

The trouble was that the Articles failed to give Congress the power to tax. As early as February 1781, Congress had proposed an amendment authorizing a 5 per cent federal duty on imports, to pay the interest and principal of the national debt. Rhode Island withheld its approval and the measure died. Two years later, when the proposal came up again in modified form, it was blocked by New York, which derived most of its income from customs duties. The nationalist Secretary of War Henry Knox exploded: "Every liberal good man is wishing New York in Hell!"

The case for giving Congress the power to tax was dramatized by the way the states paid off their own Revolutionary debts, which in 1784 came to about $21 million. Some states, including Massachusetts, liquidated their debts too quickly and taxed too heavily, thereby giving a deflationary thrust to an economic spiral already moving downward; others, including South Carolina, which had a huge per capita debt, did nothing to pay it off. Since both Confederation and state debts had been acquired in a common cause, there was a logic in treating them together. Hamilton later pressed this view upon America, but attempts to implement it roused violent factional division.

The weakness of Congress was also reflected in its inability to control shipping, to set tariffs, or in any way to wage commercial warfare on nations that discriminated against America. The coming of peace had brought a brief business boom, followed by a severe and relatively long depression. The pent-up demand for goods after the war was enormous, but was quickly met by British

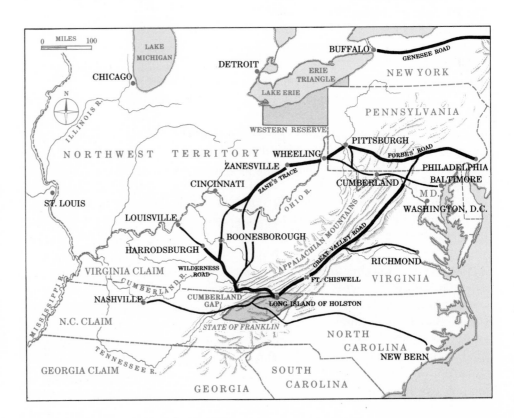

THE SETTLEMENT OF
THE WILDERNESS

By the 1780s the U.S. interior was filling with settlers and reverberating with boundary fights. The disputed areas (in gray) included the Erie Triangle, claimed by New York and Massachusetts before it went to Pennsylvania; the Western Reserve, claimed by Connecticut (it is now in Ohio); and western North Carolina, whose residents broke loose, formed the State of Franklin, and a few years later voted to return to North Carolina (the land now lies within Tennessee). The principal routes into the western regions, most of which followed Indian trails, are in black.

merchants, who dumped their products on the American market, stifling native industries and draining away precious cash. New England lost its valuable share of the British West Indies trade; the South lost its markets and prewar bounties in Britain. The states' response to these losses was not consistent: when Massachusetts, New Hampshire and Rhode Island tried to prevent the dumping of English goods, Connecticut accepted them. The depression lasted until 1787, when farm wages had fallen to 40 cents a day; commodity prices continued to sink until 1789.

I F Congress could not regulate commerce, the individual states could, and they freely used their powers against one another. New Jersey and Connecticut citizens, for example, exported most of their produce directly, but imported through such ports as Philadelphia and New York. To protect its businessmen against these imports, New Jersey levied duties on foreign goods brought in by way of other states. New York retaliated by assessing high fees on foreign goods entering from Connecticut and New Jersey. Under Pennsylvania's protective tariff of 1785, goods made in other states were technically subject to a duty, though the act was intended primarily for foreign products.

The scarcity of specie was still another source of embarrassment. Newspaper printers accepted subscriptions in salt pork; North Carolina businessmen took whiskey; Virginians fell back on their staple, tobacco. A national coinage under the decimal system was established by law in 1785, but few coins appeared until 1793. Seven of the 13 states resorted to paper money, but its value rapidly depreciated despite laws making it legal tender. Paper money was an especially vexing issue in Rhode Island, where farmers pressed the legislature to pass a law making its acceptance by reluctant merchants obligatory. In Newport a cabinetmaker named Trevett tendered paper for a bill he owed a butcher named Weeden, who would accept it only at a heavy discount from its face value. Trevett then sued Weeden under the law, but the court declared the law unconstitutional.

The effects of the depression varied widely from one state to another. The burdens of private debt were heaviest in Massachusetts, whose conservative government declined to lighten them by printing more money. By 1786, mortgage foreclosures in the state were at an all-time high; jails in central and western Massachusetts were jammed with debtors who had ample time in their dark, cramped and noisome cells to ponder the issues so many of them had fought for a few years back. Popular indignation quickly turned against lawyers who prosecuted creditors' claims—"attorneys, whose eternal gabble confounds the unexperienced rabble"—and judges who enforced these claims. Mobs sometimes prevented the courts from sitting. Town after town demanded tax reduction. "We are almost ready to cry out under the burden of our taxes as the children of Israel did in Egypt when they were required to make bricks without straw," announced the town of Coxhall, for "we cannot find that there is money enough in the town to pay."

Soon the discontented took up arms, threatening direct action. Daniel Shays, nominal commander of their "rebellion," was a man born in poverty who had finally bought a debt-burdened farm of his own. He was a veteran who had finished the Revolution a captain. Samuel Ely, a crude, uneducated, cast-off preacher, kept the pot of rebellion simmering at Northampton, while Luke Day, a demagogue and a declaimer, assumed military direction of the

The corduroy road was a familiar hazard to the hardy traveler of early America. It was constructed by laying logs side by side on trestles or across ground otherwise impassable for wagons and carriages. Though better than the backwoods trails, its washboard surface offered a bone-jarring ride.

insurgents around Springfield. Such men had neither a revolutionary ideology nor an inclination to martyrdom, and their resolve melted when it was put to the test of arms. But for most of a year they were backed by a substantial segment of the state. Behind the demagogues there were a host of supporters, including enough discontented war veterans to alarm the state's conservatives—men like Governor James Bowdoin and the Confederation's Secretary of War, Henry Knox.

To some of these conservatives, the insurrection offered a golden opportunity to increase the central government's power. Knox, for example, got Congress to approve his recommendation that federal troops be requisitioned. While ostensibly for use against the Indians in the Northwest, the men would actually be stationed in Massachusetts to deter the rebels.

In the end, Shays's Rebellion never required federal intervention. The Shaysites who attacked the Springfield arsenal were routed by a few cannon shots, and General Benjamin Lincoln, who headed the state's armed forces (equipped by funds raised by Boston businessmen), pursued the fleeing men. At Petersham, after a forced 30-mile march through a blinding snowstorm, the militia surprised the rebels, captured 150 of them and scattered the rest. Shays fled to Vermont and the revolt was virtually over. Nevertheless, the protest had elicited a good deal of sympathy among the voters. In 1787 Governor Bowdoin, who had called out the state troops, lost the election to Hancock in a landslide; meanwhile, a number of the former rebels had won seats in the Massachusetts legislature.

SHAYS's Rebellion is important, not primarily because the legislature ultimately redressed most of the rebels' grievances, but because it aroused anxiety among Federalists throughout America who felt that the country was drifting toward anarchy. "For God's sake, tell me," Washington demanded of his friends, "what is the cause of all these commotions?" He urged: "If they have *real* grievances, redress them if possible. . . . If they have not, employ the force of government against them at once." Knox, reflecting the exaggerated alarm of the property-conscious, told Washington that the Shaysites believed "that the property of the United States has been protected from confiscation of Britain by the joint exertions of *all*, and therefore ought to be the *common property* of all."

To Washington himself, the insurrection portended a desperate crisis for the nation. He wrote: "I predict the worst consequences from a half-starved, limping government, always moving upon crutches and tottering at every step . . . I do not conceive we can exist long as a nation without having lodged somewhere a power which will pervade the whole Union in as energetic a manner as the authority of the State governments extends over the several states." Other national leaders suffered similar anxieties. Thomas Jefferson's correspondents, Madison and Jay, kept reminding him of "dangerous defects" in the Confederation. "The inefficacy of our government becomes daily more and more apparent," Jay asserted.

Jefferson, physically remote in Paris, was inclined to be more cool. "I hold it that a little rebellion now and then is a good thing," he commented. And again: "The tree of liberty must be refreshed from time to time with the blood of patriots & tyrants. It is it's natural manure." Among those who shared his sentiments was New York's perennial governor, George Clinton, the defender

So sickly that he repeatedly turned down important posts, James Bowdoin still was a political leader in Massachusetts during 10 stormy years. Voted out as governor for putting down Shays's Rebellion, he emerged from retirement in 1788 to champion the Federal Constitution as the only alternative to anarchy.

Bitterly opposed to a strong central government, George Clinton, an astute politician and seven-time governor of New York, was afraid that federalization would cost him most of his vast personal power. When the change did come, however, he adapted easily and served twice as Vice President of the U.S.

of states' rights. And there were other Antifederalist leaders who were quite content with the status quo.

This is a period in American history that has generated a great deal of controversy among historians. One of them, accepting the appraisal of the Federalists, named those years "the critical period," a term that continues to be a useful description despite the efforts of more recent scholars who have tried to show that the "critical period" was really not so critical at all.

The founding fathers would have accepted without question Washington's judgment in a letter to James Madison on November 5, 1786: "We are fast verging to anarchy and confusion!" Washington was not one to sit back and let chaos take its course. With substantial holdings in the West, Washington could envision the advantages that would follow if East and West were tied together by improvements in navigation. He was aware of experiments with steam navigation, and perceived that the ability to propel boats against the current of the western rivers would make a canal connection between the headwaters of the Ohio and Potomac Rivers especially advantageous to his own state of Virginia. As president of the Potomac Company, he realized that any plan involving the navigation of the Potomac had to have the concurrence of Maryland, for the river bordered on it as well as Virginia. And Pennsylvania would have to grant permission to use the branches of the Ohio within its boundaries. Commissioners from Virginia and Maryland met at Washington's home at Mount Vernon in March 1785; and from their agreement came a proposal by Maryland that Pennsylvania and Delaware send commissioners to meet with its own and those of Virginia, and to adopt a uniform commercial system.

Madison seized on this suggestion and enlarged it: he proposed a convention of *all* states to consider commercial conditions and amend the Articles of Confederation. Five states accepted the invitation of Virginia and sent delegates to the Annapolis Convention in September 1786. None of the New England states were present. In view of the small attendance, the members of the convention adopted a report drafted by Alexander Hamilton, recommending that delegates from all the states gather at Philadelphia on the second Monday in May 1787, to propose changes "necessary to render the constitution of the federal government adequate to the exigencies of the Union. . . ." Congress reluctantly consented to calling such a meeting and, in effect, signed its own death warrant.

French foreign minister Count de Vergennes allied his country with the U.S., but could not understand American ways. In Thomas Jefferson's view, he had "very imperfect ideas of our institutions, and no confidence in them. His devotion to . . . despotism, renders him unaffectionate to our government."

Artemas Ward, once Washington's deputy commander, was "a fat old gentleman" and a judge in Massachusetts when Shays's Rebellion broke out. An ardent Federalist, he defied rioters brandishing bayonets and harangued them for two hours as traitors. This stand cost him election to Congress in 1789.

L OOKING back, it becomes evident that the bold move to impose a strong federalism on the American states and to tighten the bonds of union meant an even more radical revolution than the struggle that had brought separation from England. And the real radicals of the day, the revolutionaries, were those considered by posterity to have been the archconservatives of their time, the Federalists. These were men who had only recently been engaged in a desperate war to secure a political change. Now, to effect a change as profound, they were resolute in their determination to avoid a resort to the violence that might have erupted among the members of a loose and tenuous league wracked by centrifugal forces. Although the task before them was nearly overwhelming, the 55 men who would soon be traveling toward Philadelphia had already surmounted the first barrier to the creation of a framework of government that would long serve the new nation.

AN EARLY SETTLEMENT in Kentucky, named Boonesborough after the famed woodsman, is guarded by palisades and blockhouses. It was founded in 1775, but the settlers, busy surveying the land, did not get around to completing the fort until 1777. They finished just in time to fend off the first real Indian attacks.

A crowded path to the wilderness

ALL through the Revolution a trickle of Americans journeyed across the Appalachians into western lands once denied them by the British; after the war the flow became a flood. Newcomers to New England and the central East, finding the best of everything taken, began coiling south into what is now West Virginia and North Carolina, then turning northwest to face the forbidding mountain passes that led into the heartland. Ahead of them moved the "long hunters," so called because they were gone from home for long periods. Chief among these was Daniel Boone. A restless wagoner from North Carolina's Yadkin River Valley, he loved wild places and unlimited hunting. Boone became the region's first and widest-ranging explorer. He carved boastful records—"D Boon killed A. bar heer"—on trees all over the lower Appalachians and in Tennessee, Kentucky and Missouri. He and the others like him became the guides and defenders of the settlers who had come to tame the wild country they so loved. The woodsmen also became mighty folk heroes. Boone became the mightiest for he lived on until he was 86, spinning bigger and better yarns every year. But it was no yarn that he had led the party that cut the Wilderness Road, a path fit only for horse and rider, through the Cumberland Gap into central Kentucky, and thereby unlocked the west.

THE GREAT DANIEL BOONE is shown with gun and dog, dressed for the life of the wilderness. He was never lost, but he once admitted being "bewildered for three days."

America's armed presence appears in the West as George Rogers Clark leads his little band through 180 miles of swamp to attack the British

A BUSY RIVER PORT, Cincinnati takes its name from the Society of the Cincinnati, a group of former Revolutionary officers. New Jersey veterans founded the town, a supply point for pioneer families.

A NEW ROADWAY, carved out of the dense forests of Pennsylvania *(opposite)*, points westward like an arrow to the future. But there were long gaps, and man moved mostly on horseback or his own legs.

at Vincennes. The ice-cold water was seldom less than knee deep.

Early days of warfare and a bid for western empire

A PROMINENT figure in the westward expansion was George Rogers Clark. When he came down the Ohio into Kentucky in 1775, he was no ordinary settler. He was a Clark of Virginia, a friend of Governor Patrick Henry, with four brothers serving as officers in the Continental army. When British and Indians began raiding Kentucky, Henry placed Clark, a major in the Virginia militia, in command of the defense. Clark moved north into Illinois. By clever reconnaissance, unceasing espionage and timely ambush, he won a series of small victories. Then he made a midwinter advance on the British base at Vincennes in Indiana. As his Virginians slogged through the flooded bottom lands, many stumbled, wet their powder and were out of action—theoretically. But at Vincennes, Clark's spies sneaked out and rearmed his men from British stores, enabling them to take the town.

For want of reinforcements Clark was forced to abandon his conquests. But the peace treaty gave the land north of the Ohio back to America. Soon, on the north bank, there appeared a settlement, Losantiville. Later it would be called Cincinnati. Farther down, on the south bank, was the little town of Louisville—founded by George Rogers Clark before the Vincennes campaign.

WOODS WEALTH pours from
a wilderness sawmill which,
with its guarding blockhouse,
was built by the British north
of Saratoga in 1777. The artist, a British officer, drew this
scene from memory because
raiding Americans captured
and burned all the buildings.

A GATEWAY CITY, Pittsburgh
in 1790 is already bustling
(right) with homes, a court-
house, stocks and a pillory.
Here in 1811 a new period of
travel in the west was inau-
gurated by Nicholas Roose-
velt, who launched the first
Mississippi River steamboat.

VOYAGING CANOES, the one at left poled by an Indian brave, the other paddled by squaws, pass a newly cleared farm in this 1791 scene. The fences served two purposes for the pioneer homesteaders: they enclosed the fields and disposed of felled trees.

Watery pathways into a primitive territory

THE waterways were routes of passage. In early colonial days tiny craft beat up the tidal estuaries and into the rivers seeking new markets among the Indians, and little ships plied the coastal waters, connecting the colonies along the seaboard. Later the settlers mined the wealth of fish and waterfowl in the rivers themselves and, at the falls, found power to turn their grist- and sawmills. Along the riverbanks there were iron and coal, potash and pearlash for soap-making, tall pine for masts and every kind of lumber for planks, boards, shingles, barrel staves, house frames, and wood to feed the charcoal fires of the iron foundries of England. But it was as roadways—not always the easiest or safest routes, for water-borne travelers invited Indian attacks and snags periled the fragile craft—that the rivers played their glittering role in the growth of America. When the steamboats arrived they sped the pace of the great migration to the trackless prairies of middle America.

The hard, perilous journey
into a land of promise

A REAL wheel-bearing road was pushed over the mountains at last, and by the final years of the 18th Century, wagons were journeying north from the Carolinas through the Cumberland Gap and up the old Warriors' Path to the Ohio. Other wagons were floated down the river from Pittsburgh. In these primitive vehicles rode men of faith—men who could close their eyes and see meadows, fields of corn and fine, fat farms where now existed only unending forest, dark and dank.

Here a man's best friend was his firearm. The so-called "Kentucky rifle"—actually it was made in Pennsylvania—weighed 10 pounds. A man had to be dexterous to handle it together with his powder horn, shot pouch and patchen pouch full of wadding—all of which were called into use before the gun could be fired. The pioneer also had to keep by him a whole set of tools needed to keep his rifle in repair: a hand vise, bellows, files, screw plates. Next in importance to the rifle came the axe. Swung by strong and determined owners, it opened the forests, built the cabins and shaped the country.

A SETTLER'S CLEARING attracts a party of pioneers who pause on their way west. In the foreground are stumps of trees that have been cut down in a step preliminary to planting crops.

A TRAVELERS' RESTING PLACE provides a pause for a family on the road. The route through western Pennsylvania was long and tedious, requiring up to three months.

Cheerful French settlements on the fading frontier

BRITISH rule north of the Ohio River was only 16 years old when, with the Revolution, Americans began pressing westward. This was not long enough for English ways to override the French civilization that had existed in the area for 90 years. The French had had habitations at Chicago since 1673; Detroit, 1701; Vincennes, 1702; St. Louis, 1764. These were cheerful places. The French got along splendidly with the Indians, treated their slaves as members of the family, loved to go to Mass on Sunday mornings and dance away Sunday nights. But they were mostly rivermen, trappers and fur traders, not settling-in farmers. They sank few roots and so they eventually drifted away, leaving little more than beautiful place names to remember them by.

A new flag on the continent's western reaches

THE Revolution was but five years gone, America's western frontier still stood on the Mississippi, and the Lewis and Clark expedition into the far Northwest was still a dream in Thomas Jefferson's mind when the first American ships, *Columbia* and *Lady Washington*, explored Oregon's shores in 1788. Sea otter fur had brought them. They swapped with the Indians for pelts, then the *Columbia* under Captain Robert Gray turned westward into the Pacific. Gray sold the skins in China for tea, and then returned to Boston and sold the tea for cloth and chisels to trade with the Indians for more furs. One of the most ingenious of the Yankee traders was Joseph Ingraham, who went out as mate in *Columbia* and later commanded his own ship, the *Hope*. When the Indians did not like his cloth, Ingraham brightened it up with brass buttons. When he found no market for chisels,

he strung the tools together and sold the Indians his new and fashionable jewelry: seven-pound chisel necklaces.

The business was lucrative. In 1801 more than 14,000 pelts bought on the West Coast for cheap chisels were sold in China for $30 each. But a wealth far greater was made available to the United States by the stubbornness of Captain Gray. On a second voyage in the *Columbia* in 1792, he met Captain George Vancouver exploring in the British ship *Discovery* and suggested that all the signs indicated there must be a great river nearby. Vancouver said Gray was mistaken. So Gray turned his ship about and carefully explored the coast. On May 10, 1792, he found a noble river full of salmon which he named Columbia's River in honor of his ship. And, ignoring the rival claims of England, Spain, Russia and the Indians, he claimed all the land about for the United States.

The first national highway

The culmination of all the early road building came with the Cumberland Road, or National Turnpike. It led out of Baltimore via Cumberland, Maryland, to Ohio, Indiana and Illinois and later became U.S. Highway 40. As each segment of it was completed, herds of stock, couples in buggies and families in

light wagons were on it moving west. Swift and elegant stage-coaches swayed by on their flexing leather springs. Blue-and-red wagons, upswept at each end so the freight would not fall out on the hills, groaned ponderously behind heavy draft horses driven by cigar-smoking teamsters. Both horses and wagons had been developed in the Conestoga Valley of Pennsylvania, and took the name of the region. So did the cigars, which were first called conestogies, later shortened to stogies. With a great cracking of bull whips, stagecoach bugling and tinkling of the matched bells on the freight teams, all America was in motion.

127

6. FORGING
A NEW
REPUBLIC

ALL hopes for the future of America were centered in the Philadelphia convention when it opened in May 1787. If the convention failed to agree on a sound form of government, the young nation might never be bound together into a working union. But how to bring this about? Searching for guidance, the constitution makers who had assembled in Philadelphia studied the records of ancient Greece and Rome. They delved into the administration of the Carthaginian Republic. They looked at the systems used by aristocratic city-states like Venice and Florence, and even examined the workings of tiny federal alliances like those of Switzerland and the Netherlands. Useful parallels abounded. But the delegates soon discovered that no federal government had ever been created which both recognized the coordinate role of its member states and based its power on the consent of the people. Americans were trying to build what had never been built before.

If the Federal Convention was to succeed, the delegates would have to display a political sagacity and a talent for compromise which no comparable group of men had ever exhibited. That these men did succeed is proof of their sense of urgency and of the solid, central basis for agreement with which they began their deliberations. At the convention the political differences between the large and small states were bitter, but their differences on matters of economic interest were not acute. All the delegates were concerned, one way or another, with strengthening the central government, promoting the stability of

GEORGE WASHINGTON, in this portrait by Joseph Wright, displays the confidence and quiet strength that made him a bulwark of the Republic during its troubled early years.

property and improving the business climate. No one had to take the floor to point out the evils of cheap money or the confusion which could result when individual state laws impaired the obligation of contracts. The framers of the Constitution were not doctrinaire theoreticians, but practical realists. John Dickinson perhaps best expressed their temper when he observed that "experience must be our only guide. Reason may mislead us."

WATCHING the proceedings with fascination from Paris, American minister Thomas Jefferson once referred to the historic convention at Philadelphia as "an assembly of demi-gods." Actually the 55 delegates were very realistic humans, most of them men of exceptional talent and experience, which were to stand them and the new nation in good stead.

Despite this formidable array of talent, the new Constitution might never have received public approval if George Washington had not taken part in the proceedings. He had announced his intention of remaining in retirement, and was beset with all sorts of personal problems. But after surviving the years of war and hardship, Washington was determined that the colonies should not now founder. On May 9 he left Mount Vernon for Philadelphia, where he was to serve throughout the convention as its dignified presiding officer.

Along with Washington, a dazzling group represented Virginia. It included the author of Virginia's Bill of Rights, George Mason, who viewed strong governments with deep distrust; the colony's young governor, Edmund Randolph; and James Madison, the directing intelligence of the delegation. Slight, diffident and weak of voice, the 36-year-old Madison day to day demonstrated the incisive quality of his mind and the audacious reach of his Federalist vision. He also kept a private journal of the secret proceedings, which provided posterity with an illuminating account of what went on backstage.

In prestige and ability the Pennsylvania delegation was a fair match for Virginia's. Franklin's 81 years had not dimmed his enthusiasm for the experiment of a democratic republic. His fellow delegates included James Wilson, the same lawyer who eight years earlier had come under attack for his activities as a speculator, but nevertheless a man whose original mind and oratorical talents decisively helped the Federalist cause at critical moments; financier Robert Morris, a man of much power but few words; and debonair Gouverneur Morris, who could shock the sober assembly with flashes of naked cynicism.

In choosing its delegates the strongly Antifederalist New York legislature passed over John Jay in favor of two mediocre upstaters, Robert Yates and John Lansing; Alexander Hamilton was included as a concession to downstate Federalist opinion. South Carolina sent its wartime governor John Rutledge and the two Pinckneys, Charles and his cousin Charles Cotesworth. The small states had some notable champions, too: New Jersey's great governor William Livingston, and William Paterson, the state's Revolutionary attorney general; Delaware's able John Dickinson; Connecticut's capable Roger Sherman.

Not many Antifederalists attended the convention at all. Outstanding men like Patrick Henry (who said he "smelt a rat") and Richard Henry Lee refused to represent Virginia. With men of this persuasion absent, there was only one basic compromise that had to be worked out—the resolution of the struggle between the small states and the large ones over which would control the new government. This was the first substantive matter raised. After quickly agreeing on procedural rules for the convention (the vote was to be by states, with

There was a tender side to James Madison, "Father of the Constitution," whose Virginia plan was the basis for the final document. At 31 he fell in love with a 15-year-old girl, ran up large bills at the barber's and was desolated when she jilted him. As a cure, Jefferson recommended "firmness of mind."

Gouty aristocrat George Mason, "Father of the Bill of Rights," who hoped to leave his sons "a Crust of Bread and Liberty," said the Constitution was not democratic enough. A fiery orator, he was not completely reconciled even after the first 10 amendments, based on his own Virginia laws, were adopted.

each having one vote under a simple majority rule), the delegates turned to the Virginia plan presented by Edmund Randolph but believed to have been drawn up by Madison. It proposed a government truly national in form with a legislature of two houses, the lower to be elected by the people, the upper to be chosen by the lower house from persons named by the state legislatures. This body was to make laws "in all cases to which the separate States are incompetent," and could nullify all state laws contrary to the Constitution. A "National Executive" was to be chosen by the legislature, was to have all the executive powers possessed by the Congress under the old Confederation and would serve for an unspecified term of years. There would be a federal judicial system, and the executive, acting with federal judges, would have veto power over the acts of the legislative body and could review the laws of the states.

In broad outline the Virginia plan served as the basis for the Constitution as eventually adopted. But strong disagreement over how it would work led to quarreling and quick counterproposals. Some of the delegates did not think the proposed government had power enough; others, that it had too much. Hardly had debate on the plan begun when Edmund Randolph moved "that a *national* Government ought to be established consisting of a *supreme* Legislative, Executive and Judiciary." Gouverneur Morris, joining him in the proposal, warned, "We had better take a supreme government now than a despot twenty years hence—for come he must."

The small states were not much worried by Morris' vision of a future dictatorship; they feared they would be completely outvoted by a few large states under the Virginia plan's proposal to apportion seats in the national legislature according to taxes paid or according to free population. New Jersey therefore came forward with a small-state counterplan for a one-house legislature in which each state would be equally represented regardless of population, with a plural executive to be chosen by Congress. The New Jersey plan would in substance have continued the old Articles of Confederation, except that it gave the Congress the right to tax and to regulate commerce.

In the midst of the intense debate that followed over the two plans, Alexander Hamilton presented his own extreme nationalist proposals, which received no support but may have prepared the way for acceptance of the more moderate Virginia plan. Then the convention agreed on a lower house, popularly elected, and an upper chamber made up of men elected by the various state legislatures, a mild revision of the Virginia plan.

Duridurnng the debate over proportionate representation versus state equality in the two legislative chambers, the rivalry between large and small states flared more violently than before. For two days Luther Martin of Maryland harangued the convention, asserting that state equality was "essential to the federal idea" and that the central government existed merely to preserve the states. Madison pointed out that the small states had no real need to fear a combination of large states against them, since the economic interests of the latter were too diverse to lead to solid coalition. The discussion grew more animated. Franklin, though a freethinker, proposed that a clergyman be invited to offer calming prayers to open each session. In reply, Hamilton is said to have snapped that the convention could transact its business without "the necessity of calling in foreign aid."

To ease the tension Roger Sherman suggested the convention give each

Rufus King, affable, wealthy and wise, was a prominent New York politician and one of the most influential of the secondary leaders at the convention. A moderate on everything but slavery, which he abominated, he was first in favor of a weak central government and wound up favoring a strong one.

Luther Martin of Maryland, the "rollicking . . . reprobate genius," had a terrible temper, which he exercised liberally at the convention. When his arguments for a weak government were rejected, he tried to scuttle the Constitution—but not before he suggested that federal treaties transcend state laws.

131

state, large and small, an equal vote in the Senate, but keep proportionate representation in the lower house. Known as the Connecticut compromise, because it was solidly supported by that state along with a number of other small states, Sherman's proposition was condemned by the Federalists as a surrender to the principle of states' rights. They fought it fiercely. "This country must be united," Gouverneur Morris warned. "If persuasion does not unite it, the sword will."

The vote was a tie. Then a special committee with one member from each state, a composition decidedly favorable to the small-state bloc, recommended that in the lower house each state should be represented in proportion to population (with slaves counted at three fifths of their total number) and that in the upper house each should have an equal vote. The lower house alone would have the power to originate money bills. This crucial proposal carried, but only by a bare five states to four.

Along with this major compromise went a cluster of small ones. The South agreed to give Congress the power to pass navigation acts which the North wanted; in turn the North, after some argument, agreed to prohibit Congress from interfering with the slave trade for 20 years. The upper South would actually have preferred an immediate end to the trade, and George Mason of Virginia warned prophetically that "by an inevitable chain of causes and effects providence punishes national sins by national calamities."

There were innumerable other adjustments to be made. Wilson first proposed direct election of the executive by all the people. George Mason declared that such a thing would be as unnatural as asking a blind man to pick out colors. Wilson then hit upon the ingenious system of presidential electors. This electoral compromise proved in the long run to be a victory for both federalism and democracy, for nearly all the states eventually arranged that presidential electors had to be chosen directly by the voters, with the electors reduced to figureheads. The presidential term was also a sensible compromise, for some delegates wanted a life term; others, seven years; still others, a three-year term without eligibility for re-election. The delegates fixed on four years without limiting the President's right to run again.

Another decision settled the significant question of who could declare state laws unconstitutional. Even the Federalist Gouverneur Morris agreed that to give such power to Congress would create a threat "terrible to the states." And oddly enough, it was not a nationalist but a states' rights man, Luther Martin, who proposed the clause that made the Constitution and the laws and treaties of the United States binding upon the judges in every state. Since the Judiciary Act of 1789, enacted by the first Congress under the new Constitution, was to provide for appeals from state courts to the federal judiciary, this clause became a cornerstone of national sovereignty.

I N retrospect the basic agreements among the convention delegates seem more important than the more highly publicized differences. The proceedings of the convention also showed how quickly the old colonies were willing to grant their new, self-chosen government powers the mere assertion of which by England had triggered furious outcries. The inability to raise taxes had crippled the old Continental Congress; both the Virginia and New Jersey plans granted Congress power to levy and collect them. When the tax proposal was put to a vote, it carried with no state dissenting. The convention

The first coin struck for the U.S. in 1787 was the so-called Fugio Cent. On one side are 13 circles representing the union. On the other, the word "Fugio" is next to a sundial to show that time flies. Then, in place of the latter-day motto, "In God We Trust," appears a sensible admonition, "Mind Your Business," believed to have been suggested by Benjamin Franklin.

unanimously granted Congress the power to pay national debts and "provide for the common defense and general welfare of the United States," one of the most significant nationalist clauses. Every proposed plan granted Congress the power to regulate commerce, both with foreign nations and between states. A large majority of the delegates favored (and put into the Constitution) a prohibition against the issue of paper money by the states, the same prohibition that England tried so long to enforce.

The pace of the convention is impressive evidence of the ability of the delegates to come to terms with one another and to get work done. The convention opened on May 25. By July 26 a basic plan for the Constitution had been adopted and sent to a Committee of Detail. That committee swiftly presented a draft version which was debated clause by clause from August 6 until September 10, when the Constitution was agreed upon and referred to a Committee of Style for finishing touches. The Committee of Style presented the final draft for approval on September 12. On September 17 the convention happily adjourned, as Washington noted in his diary, "to the City Tavern." There the delegates dined contentedly together and then said goodby to one another.

As president of the convention, George Washington seldom took part in the debates. But after the daily sessions were over, he joined with the delegates to evolve wise compromises. At odd moments, he managed a measure of fun, attending concerts, poetry readings, even a lecture on "The Power of Eloquence," from which, during the convention, he suffered aplenty.

Now that the first part of their task was done, the framers faced the even harder job of securing approval for their work. They had ignored their instructions by drawing up a new Constitution instead of merely proposing amendments to the old one (prompting Elbridge Gerry, a wealthy Massachusetts Antifederalist delegate, to refer to the work of the convention sneeringly as that "fraudulent usurpation of Philadelphia"). The convention members were understandably reluctant now to submit their plan to the Confederation Congress for approval.

The convention had further defied the Continental Congress by deciding that ratification by any nine of the 13 states would be sufficient "for the Establishment of this Constitution between the States so ratifying the Same." Thus, over considerable angry protest, the convention bypassed the Congress. With a sensitive appreciation of the national and revolutionary feeling involved, Gouverneur Morris had changed the draft wording of the Preamble from "We the people of the States of New Hampshire, Massachusetts," etc., to read "We the People of the United States." Out of the four months of wrangling between large and small states, between nationalists and states' righters, between opposing sections and rival interest groups, the delegates had emerged with their conception of the collective good of the people as a controlling aim. So it was sound judgment for the convention to avoid debate by state legislatures biased toward state sovereignty. It was revolutionary to ask the legislatures to submit the Constitution to all the people for ratification, a method previously used only by Massachusetts in 1780.

The country at large was far more sharply divided over the Constitution than were the delegates sent to Philadelphia. Commercial and manufacturing interests, both along the seaboard and in the interior, creditors, Revolutionary officers and professional men were quick to support the new instrument. But states' righters, agrarians, paper money men, various types of debtors and many other special-interest blocs were outraged by it.

The Federalist backers of the Constitution had one great advantage: they came with a concrete proposal. Their opponents, the Antifederalists, were forced to oppose something with almost nothing. The objections to the strong

South Carolina's General Charles Cotesworth Pinckney, the graver of the two Pinckneys at the convention, proposed the ban on religious tests for public offices. His philandering cousin Charles was far more active in the Constitutional debate. Longtime friends, the two men later broke over politics.

Proud blood flowed in the veins of "Light-Horse Harry" Lee, Washington's brilliant cavalry general and a remote descendant of Lady Godiva of Coventry, who also rode horses. After the war Lee fought hard to get his state into the union, as hard as his son, Robert E. Lee, was to fight to get it out again.

Constitution, however sincere, inevitably sounded weak and obstructive, not constructive. In practical terms the Antifederalists stood for a one-house legislature, a popularly elected judiciary, a weak executive and little else. Their claim to be the more democratic of the parties might have brought them wide popular support, but many of the Antifederalists were plainly as distrustful of the masses as were their opponents. One of their leaders, George Clinton, governor of New York, criticized the people for their fickle tendency "to vibrate from one extreme to another." Elbridge Gerry, who had asserted in the convention that "the evils we experience flow from the excess of democracy," was loudly concerned about "the danger of the levelling spirit."

It is true that the Antifederalists *did* worry more about the threat posed to individual liberties by the leviathan state. The Federalists, less concerned, felt the immediate problem was to give the central government more power and energy. But in fact the Antifederalists often looked very much like a group of state and local officeholders concerned about their vested interests. Fortunately for the evolution of representative democracy in America, the principles of the conservative revolutionaries (who framed the Constitution) and their so-called democratic opponents (who preferred the *status quo*) complemented each other.

WHEN it came to ratification, the roles played by the small and large states during the convention were reversed. The little states had vehemently resisted strong central government. Now they quickly fell in line, reassured by the crucial Connecticut compromise, which gave them an advantage beyond their numbers or wealth. Delaware, New Jersey, Connecticut and Georgia were among the earliest to approve the document.

The main battles against ratifying the Constitution were fought in the larger states. Trouble first came in powerful Pennsylvania. There the Antifederalists frantically worked for a delay. The Federalists responded with rough tactics and driving urgency. Their strategy paid immediate dividends, for the convention adopted the Constitution 46 to 23. The struggle in Pennsylvania revealed a division which was to be repeated throughout the country. The large commercial cities, like Philadelphia, were for the Constitution. Farm areas, especially to the west, were opposed. Inevitably a class antagonism came into the controversy. Antifederalists were soon asking if the *"low born"* were going to stand by and allow the "600 well born" in the entire country to ram this document down their throats.

For a time that seemed to be exactly what would happen. In Massachusetts the infuriated but disorganized and leaderless opponents of the Constitution fought noisily and with vigor. "These lawyers and men of learning and moneyed men," cried Amos Singletary, an Antifederalist farmer, "that talk so finely, and gloss over matters so smoothly, to make us poor illiterate people swallow down the pill, expect to get into Congress themselves . . . and get all the power and all the money into their own hands, and then they will swallow up all us little folks. . . ." In the end the Constitution won in Massachusetts by only 19 votes out of 355, but the grim struggle brought about significant concessions. Many state ratifying conventions urged that before final adoption certain protective amendments be added to the Constitution.

"The plot thickens fast," Washington wrote to Lafayette on May 28, 1788. "A few short weeks will determine the political fate of America." Eight states, just one short of the number required for establishment of the Constitution, had already ratified. The issue was finally settled in two special conventions, one in Richmond, Virginia, the other in Poughkeepsie, New York.

In Virginia both sides had strained every nerve to see that their own men were sent to the ratifying convention. Washington thought the Antifederalists had used "every art that could inflame the passions or touch the interest of men." Opponents of the Constitution claimed that the government, once established, would tax the poor man's property out of existence and give away the Mississippi. The Federalists countered by citing the names of their leaders, men of prestige and strong talents: Washington himself, "Light-Horse Harry" Lee, Madison, John Marshall. Even so, Virginia's Federalists soon realized they faced an uphill battle. Patrick Henry, their chief antagonist, claimed that "four-fifths of our inhabitants are opposed to the new scheme of government." Sure of this support, delegates like Henry, George Mason and Richard Henry Lee arranged to contest the Constitution point by point. This was a fatal error. Prolonged discussions played into the hands of the Federalists, who did not have the numerical strength at the convention to risk a quick vote, but did have outstanding advocates whose skill and persuasion could sway votes in floor debate.

The meeting had hardly begun when the Federalists sprang their surprise. All along the Antifederalists had counted on Governor Edmund Randolph, who had left Philadelphia without signing the Constitution. To their consternation he warned that the world looked upon Americans "as little wanton bees, who had played for liberty, but had no sufficient solidity or wisdom" to keep it. Then he announced dramatically, "I am a friend to the Union."

Madison argued the Constitution on its merits, clause by clause. The young lawyer John Marshall defended its judiciary provisions. In reply the Antifederalists resorted to reckless assertions and personal vilification. To Patrick Henry the Constitution was a threat to liberty, the large standing army it would require was a threat to peace. As for the "great and mighty President," he sounded like a monarch. "The purse is gone," Henry lamented, "the sword is gone," and now, he said, the nation was about to lose the scales of justice. In a closing speech Henry warned that the happiness of one half of the human race depended on what was decided—and as if to bear him out a sudden storm interrupted him. Darkness closed in, thunder crashed, lightning struck close to the assembly building, lending dramatic support to Henry's oratory.

At the vote, the Constitution carried by 89 to 79. To conciliate the opposition and meet its most valid criticisms, the convention coupled ratification with a proposal that certain amendments be made to the Constitution. When the new Congress first met in 1789, James Madison offered a group of amendments; 10 of them—the Bill of Rights—were later approved by the states.

IN New York the outnumbered Federalists, expecting an onslaught directed by Governor George Clinton, chief of the Antifederalist forces, seized the offensive months before the ratifying convention opened. On October 27, 1787, a series of 85 letters began appearing in New York newspapers under the pseudonym of "Publius." In May 1788 the letters were published in book form as *The Federalist*. It later came out that John Jay, James Madison and Alexander Hamilton had written the papers. These brilliant essays, still the classic exposition of the Constitution, exposed the Confederation's weakness

No man spoke more often in the convention than peg-legged Gouverneur Morris of Pennsylvania. "Give the votes to the [poor]," he warned, "and they will sell them to the rich." But when his own antidemocratic ideas were finally defeated, he rephrased the Constitution in his own majestic prose.

Oliver Ellsworth of Connecticut was a deep-thinking man whose family could determine the depth of his thought by the amount of snuff he spilled on the floor. At the convention it was he who original- ly suggested that the name "United States" replace the word "nation- al" in the body of the Constitution.

Chief Justice John Marshall took a drink now and then. But accord- ing to one story, he became so wor- ried about drunken judges that he and members of his court shunned drink except in rainy weather. Aft- er the Louisiana Purchase, it was dry in Washington but they ruled that it must be raining somewhere.

while demonstrating "the utility of the Union to your political prosperity."

Hamilton's final *Federalist* letter declared: "A *Nation* without a *National Government* is, in my view, an awful spectacle. The establishment of a con- stitution, in time of profound peace, by the voluntary consent of a whole peo- ple, is a *prodigy*, to the completion of which I look forward with trembling anxiety." He had every reason for anxiety, for despite the reasoned arguments of the *Federalist* papers, the Poughkeepsie convention was extremely hostile to the Constitution. The upstate Antifederalists commanded a clear majority. Hamilton determined to play for time, realizing that the only hope lay in full discussion which might modify opposition.

Time aided the Federalists in another way. During the six sizzling summer weeks in which Hamilton harangued the convention in Poughkeepsie, the magic number of nine ratifying states was reached elsewhere. On June 21, 1788, New Hampshire, the ninth state, ratified; Virginia followed four days later. It became evident to the New York delegates that no matter what they did the new instrument of government would automatically go into effect. And Melancton Smith, leading upstate opponent of the Constitution, rose to con- cede that he had been convinced by the Federalists, a tribute either to Ham- ilton's eloquence or to John Jay's threat that if the state withheld approval, New York City would secede and ratify on its own. The Constitution was ap- proved by a slim three votes.

Eleven states were now in the Union. Two stayed out for a time. North Car- olina had to hold a second convention before approval was voted in Novem- ber 1789. Rhode Island, which had boycotted the Philadelphia convention, did not decide to join the Union until May 1790.

ALTHOUGH the strengthening of the Federal Union was the result of a revo- lution in the political thinking of Americans, it has not always been so regarded by critics of the Constitution. A theory once prevalent among his- torians described the Constitution as "counterrevolutionary" in aim, de- signed by men who feared democracy and schemed for checks, balances and division of powers to curb majority rule. Even granting that the founding fa- thers were tough-minded men of affairs, who expected to, and did, prosper under the new Constitution, still this theory oversimplifies both their mo- tives and their interests. The commercial interests of Federalist manufactur- ers and importers, land speculators and wheat farmers were so diverse as to largely cancel each other out. Moreover, the economic interests of the Anti- federalists were very little different from those of their opponents; with property ownership at the time already widespread, the founding fathers were governed by principles as well as by their pocketbooks.

Whatever the reasons which seem, in retrospect, to have motivated the framing of the Constitution, Americans of 1788 greeted its ratification with relief and enthusiasm. Boston, Charleston and New York outdid one another in celebrating ratification with fetes and processions, but Philadelphia outdid them all in ardor and ingenuity. When the post brought news that Virginia had at last gone Federal, it ended the tormenting doubts about what course the country would take. The city fathers determined that the Fourth of July should be the occasion for a magnificent display of the new Federal spirit.

As dawn rose over the Delaware, the ship *Rising Sun* fired a national salute. While the bells of Christ Church rang out, each of 10 gaily decorated vessels anchored in the harbor hoisted a pennant representing each of the 10 states that had ratified. There were elaborate floats, and richly dressed horsemen —representing epic events which had led to the recent independence and the new Constitution—jostled one another in triumphal progress down Market Street. A huge dome supported by 13 Corinthian columns depicted "The Federal Edifice." Appropriately enough, the high point of the parade was the float showing the Federal ship *Union*, created by decorating a barge from the ship *Alliance*, which had been taken by John Paul Jones in the memorable fight against the *Serapis*.

Bricklayers carried a pennant with the punned motto "Both Buildings and Rulers are the Works of our hands," and all the other trades and professions, masters and journeymen alike, joined in too. Benjamin Rush, the patriot physician, told how 17 clergymen "of the most dissimilar religious principles" marched together. "The Rabbi of the Jews locked in the arms of two ministers of the gospel was a most delightful sight," he reported joyfully. "There could not have been a more happy emblem [for] that section of the new Constitution which opens all its power and offices alike not only to every sect of Christians but to worthy men of *every* religion." James Wilson, who had helped so much in the framing of the Constitution, made the solemn commemoration address. One of the signers of the Declaration, Francis Hopkinson, not only planned the celebration, but wrote a commemoratory ode which was scattered among the crowd. Even the weather seemed propitious. A cool breeze blew throughout the day, and the evening sky was lit by the aurora borealis. "Heaven," remarked the enthusiasts, "was on the federal side of the question." Dr. Rush, an early temperance crusader, rejoiced that the 17,000 gathered on the green drank nothing more intoxicating than beer and cider during 10 toasts in honor of the 10 ratifying states. He expressed the pious hope that citizens would soon learn "to despise spirituous liquors as Anti-federal."

If Dr. Rush's fellow citizens did not necessarily follow his counsel to do their drinking along strictly party lines, they did, both then and in coming decades, share some of his vision and patriotic ardor. Summing it all up, the Philadelphia physician-statesman wrote to John Adams that the Constitution

> has a thousand . . . things to recommend it. It makes us a nation. It rescues us from anarchy and slavery. It revives agriculture and commerce. It checks moral and political iniquity. In a word, it makes a man both willing to *live* and to *die*. To *live*, because it opens to him fair prospects of great public and private happiness. To *die*, because it ensures peace, order, safety and prosperity to his children.

New York erupted in celebration in July 1788. Five thousand men marched in a parade, along with such elegant floats as the frigate "Hamilton" above. Six thousand sat down to a monster feast and drank numerous toasts—for nine states had ratified the Constitution. The United States was born.

BENJAMIN RUSH had seen a dream come true. He had lived to see a colonial people win their freedom. He had witnessed the birth of a nation. He had shared with his contemporaries the agonies that attended the launching of the new republic. Although the founding fathers had feared that independence was incompatible with centralized authority, they had bowed to necessity and had created a federal structure that endowed the national government with both power and energy while safeguarding individual liberty and traditional authority. The resilient and durable instrument of government which they fashioned stands almost two centuries later as the epitome of all that is admirable in the American spirit, as a statement of purpose that serves as an inspiration to all those yearning for a decent life.

A country squire's career of service

A^T home all day alone. Wind at East and very Cloudy all day." This was all that George Washington wrote in his diary for March 16, 1797, his first full day back at Mount Vernon after eight years as President. But beneath this habitual reserve, Washington, who was really an emotional man, rejoiced that his frustrating absences were over. His love for Mount Vernon began while his older brother owned it. First as a farmboy visitor, later as proprietor, Washington had aspired to and enjoyed the gracious life of the country squire; but the squire's code of duty and honor came into conflict with private pursuits and domestic happiness. His first work, surveying, took him away from home for extended periods. His military career kept him away through much of the 1750s. The experience he gained fighting the Indians and the French won him a post he had not sought—Commander-in-Chief of the Continental Army. After the Revolution was won, the nation had called on him to serve two terms as President. But now his tasks were finished, and the squire of Mount Vernon was home to stay.

On the pages that follow are photographs of Mount Vernon and of other places indissolubly associated with George Washington. These pictures, taken by Nina Leen of LIFE, employ an imaginative, impressionistic technique to re-create the spirit of a time long gone by—the dawn of the United States.

AT SPORT among the gentry, youthful Washington rides to hounds with well-connected George William Fairfax. In 1748, when Washington was 16, the friends took a wondrous journey over the Blue Ridge to survey Fairfax lands in virgin Shenandoah Valley.

A SURVEYING COMPASS used in Washington's early career stands (*opposite*) over a colonial tricorne at Mount Vernon. George surveyed this forest for practice when he was 15.

From a rustic boyhood to the world of the gentry

RIVERSIDE fields, a strip of woodland, a cluster of outbuildings around a plain eight-room house—this was Ferry Farm, where George Washington's family went to live in 1738, when he was six. Almost from the first, the farm interested George less than the ferry which docked nearby, less than Fredericksburg, across the Rappahannock, the first town he had ever seen. A few years later, his thoughts were ranging far beyond his homely chores and sketchy lessons; he spent more and more time at Mount Vernon, the fine estate of his beloved brother Lawrence, and he drank in the worldly talk of a polished gentry—soldiers, sportsmen, planters. After 1743, when his father died, his mother, a simple woman of rustic ways, stayed on at Ferry Farm. George returned there to pay her respectful visits, but he had moved on to the great glittering world of Mount Vernon.

A TOWN HOUSE in Fredericksburg (above) is the home to which Washington brought his mother from Ferry Farm in 1772. Hedges (right) line the path he took on visits.

THE MUDDY RAPPAHANNOCK, clear and brisk when young Washington rode his horse on its banks, now flows lazily past a clearing that was part of his Ferry Farm home.

141

VEST AND CANE that belonged to Washington are displayed in the Mount Vernon library. Behind is a book "press" with many volumes on his chief interests, military science and agriculture.

COSTLY HARPSICHORD, which Washington imported for Nelly Custis, stands in the parlor. Her brother, who probably played the flute, recalled that she would practice for hours on end.

Mount Vernon and its family in the years of growth

IN 1754, when George Washington leased Mount Vernon from the family of his late brother Lawrence, the house was a square, one-and-a-half-story structure. Although he did not inherit the estate until 1761, Washington built up the house to two and a half stories before 1759, when, preceded by orders to spruce up the rooms and polish the staircase (opposite), he arrived with his bride, the widow Martha Custis. Martha brought him a fortune and, more important to making Mount Vernon a home, her two young children. The new family (below) knit well: with George and Martha remaining childless, he took her Patsy and Jack to his heart; and when Jack died he adopted Jack's two youngest children, Nelly and George. Before the grandchildren were born, Mount Vernon had assumed its present outlines with the addition of two wings. Young George grew up a charming idler, content to bask in the glory of his great namesake. Nelly, whose abilities rivaled her beauty, was Washington's pride and delight; and when she married his favorite nephew, Lawrence Lewis, the squire of Mount Vernon promised them 2,000 of his acres for their own estate.

GEMLIKE MINIATURES show three generations of the Washingtons. George and Martha (top) outlived her own children (middle), raised her son's (bottom).

FROM THE MAIN HALL, Mount Vernon's front door opens onto rolling green lawns, and its burnished stairway (opposite) leads up to five bedrooms and Washington's suite.

A genteel assortment
of pleasures and pastimes

As serious and reserved as Washington was, he had many moments of gay relaxation. At his table he chatted freely, laughed heartily and enjoyed a glass of wine—often two or three. He spent freely on fine clothes in the latest fashion to set off a physique which he described to one London tailor as: "6 feet high and proportionately made; if anything rather slender than thick . . . with pretty long Arms and thighs." Confident in his taste and carriage, he indulged his fondness for dancing at every opportunity, with something like abandon. Often he rollicked through every dance; once he raised eyebrows by monopolizing the lovely wife of General Greene.

He liked to gamble. His wagering ranged from a few shillings on his skill at billiards, to several pounds in raffles and racing purses, to outright plunging in lotteries, a common business form of the day. But his passion was cards: lanterloo *(below)*, whist and quadrille. Characteristically, he played a cautious game and kept a meticulous record of his winnings and losses. Over all, he lost a little each year—just enough to add a touch of asperity to the advice he sent his sportive nephew Bushrod Washington: "gaming" should be shunned as ". . . the child of Avarice, the brother of iniquity, and father of Mischief."

FOUR HANDS OF LANTERLOO, Washington's favorite pastime, are dealt out on his card table *(below)* in Mount Vernon's west parlor. This old game combined elements of poker and hearts.

A GRACIOUS SETTING for gaiety and elegance, the ballroom of Gadsby's Tavern in Alexandria, Virginia, is reproduced with its musicians' balcony as a display in New York's Metropolitan

Museum of Art. In the custom of their time, George and Martha Washington did not stage balls at home; but as members of the Alexandria Assembly, a club which sponsored regional dances, they attended many in town. These functions graced the City Tavern until 1792, when a larger hall was built next door. Great balls at Gadsby's honored Washington on his last two birthdays.

Eight years of absence and the burdens of command

ON June 18, 1775, George Washington wrote his wife Martha that Congress had named him commander-in-chief of the colonial forces: "so far from seeking this appointment, I have used every endeavor in my power to avoid it . . . from a consciousness of its being too great a trust for my capacity. . . ." He assured her, ". . . I shall return safe to you in the fall"; but except for two brief stopovers in 1781, he would be away from Mount Vernon for more than eight years.

Through that desperate epoch, Washington presided over Mount Vernon by mail. His instructions detailed the smallest repair, the best use of a particular slave. They were also sweeping. A letter to his nephew-caretaker declared: "Let the Hospitality of the House, with respect to the poor be kept up; Let no one go hungry away . . . I have no objection to your giving my money in Charity, to the Amount of forty or fifty Pounds a Year. . . ."

Finally the war ended, and at noon on December 4, 1783, George Washington bade farewell to arms in New York's Fraunces Tavern (opposite). After a long silence, he told his officers: "With a heart full of love and gratitude, I now take leave of you. I most devoutly wish that your later days may be as prosperous and happy as your former ones have been glorious and honorable."

Then he began his journey home to Mount Vernon.

A HOMEY PARLOR is a historical site in the Webb House in Wethersfield, Connecticut. On May 21-23, 1781, Washington met here with France's Rochambeau to draw a plan for the Yorktown campaign.

A HUGE HEARTH dominates the kitchen of the Ford House in Morristown, New Jersey. Around its fire, Washington and his staff huddled in 1779-1780, through a winter worse than Valley Forge, 1777-1778.

GLEAMING WINEGLASSES conjure up the farewell toast that was drunk in 1783 at this table in Fraunces Tavern, still serving meals in downtown New York. His glass held aloft, Washington bade his comrades "come and take me by the hand." Then he stood "suffused in tears" as each of 40-odd officers "marched up to, kissed, and parted with his General-in-Chief."

"The history of a day" back home at Mount Vernon

ON December 24, 1783, after a triumphal trip, Washington arrived home and settled down to a simple routine. "I begin my diurnal course with the sun," he wrote a friend. He would then inspect his estate and note the deterioration "which my buildings have sustained by an absence and neglect of eight years. . . . [Then] breakfast (a little after seven o'clock) is ready." Until dinner at midafternoon he rode around his farms. "The usual time of sitting at table, a walk, and tea [*right*], brings me within the dawn of candlelight"—and early retirement. "Having given you the history of a day," Washington ended, "it will serve for a year. . . ."

ON A DRESSING TABLE in the master bedroom lie Martha Washington's accessories in neat array. After completing her toilette, Martha joined her early-rising husband for breakfast.

ON THE PIAZZA, a late tea is set out, featuring a fruitcake baked to Martha's own recipe. Served at 7 p.m., this outdoor meal was often the Washingtons' last meal of the day.

BENEATH A PECAN TREE, Mount Vernon's cookhouse flanks the mansion to the left front. Between this outbuilding and the butler's house *(upper right)* is a lane that Washington often took on his way to and from the stable. Opposite lay slave quarters and a cobbler's shop.

NEAR THE GREENHOUSE, to the right of the mansion, is the flower garden, still planted to Washington's design. In 1798, one visitor noted that the garden "is well cultivated, perfectly kept . . . quite in English style . . . [although] the General has never left America. . . ."

149

The general's "retirement"

In 1784, five weeks after his return to Mount Vernon, Washington wrote to his recent comrade-in-arms, Lafayette: "At length . . . I am become a private citizen, on the banks of the Potomac [*left, above*], and under the shadow of my own Vine and my own Fig-tree, free from the bustle of a camp. . . . I am not

only retired from all public employments, but I am retiring within myself; and shall be able to view the solitary walk, and tread the paths of private life with a heartfelt satisfaction."

The pleasures of home and solitude were frequently broken by uninvited guests. Washington later wrote that these stran-gers said they came "out of respect to me," but "Pray, would not the word curiosity answer as well?" Yet all too soon for the country squire, the interruptions ended. On April 16, 1789, he "bade adieu to Mount Vernon, to private life and to domes-tic felicity," and left to take up the duties of the presidency.

CHRONOLOGY A timetable of American and world events: 1775-1789

WORLD EVENTS	TERRITORIAL EXPANSION	POLITICS	MILITARY	ECONOMICS and SCIENCE	RELIGION, ARTS and PEOPLE
1740-80 Maria Theresa of Austria reigns as "king" of Hungary	**1774-76** Spaniards explore northwest Pacific coast to counter British and Russians	**Feb. 1775** House of Lords rejects Chatham's conciliation plan	**Apr. 1775** British order General Gage to use force, if necessary, to carry out acts of Parliament	**1774-76** Smallpox prevalent throughout colonies	**1771-90** Franklin writes his autobiography
1740-86 Frederick the Great reigns in Prussia		**Feb. 1775** Parliament declares Massachusetts in state of rebellion	**Apr. 1775** Minutemen fight British at Lexington and Concord	**1775** Congress establishes postal system for United Colonies; Franklin appointed Postmaster General	**1775** Quakers establish first antislavery society in U.S.
1759-88 Charles III reigns in Spain		**Feb. 1775** House of Commons endorses Lord North's conciliation plan	**May 1775** Americans capture Fort Ticonderoga	**1775** John Jones writes first American textbook on surgery, *Remarks on the Treatment of Wounds and Fractures*	**1775 onward:** Charles Willson Peale paints Revolutionary portraits
1760-1820 George III reigns in England	**1775** Transylvania Company acquires large area in western Kentucky by treaty with the Cherokees	**Mar. 1775** Parliament passes New England Restraining Act	**June 1775** Congress names Washington chief of Continental forces	**1775-76** David Bushnell builds first American submarine	**1775-82** Poet John Trumbull writes "M'Fingal," a satire on Tories
1762-96 Catherine the Great reigns in Russia		**Mar. 1775** Patrick Henry makes his "Liberty or Death" speech before Virginia Assembly	**June 1775** British drive Americans off Bunker Hill	**1775-83** American trade with Britain sinks to 5 per cent of prewar level	**1775-83** States reform prison systems, penal codes, education
1774-92 Louis XVI reigns in France	**1775** Daniel Boone blazes Wilderness Trail, founds Boonesborough	**May 1775** Second Continental Congress meets in Philadelphia	**July 1775-Mar. 1776** Siege of Boston		**1775-84** Philip Freneau writes patriotic poems
1775 England hires German mercenaries to fight Americans		**May 1775** Mecklenburg County (North Carolina) Resolutions annul laws of Parliament and king	**Aug.-Dec. 1775** Montgomery and Arnold lead expedition against Quebec		
1775-83 European nations become involved in American War of Independence		**July 1775** Congress adopts Olive Branch Petition and rejects Lord North's conciliation plan	**Dec. 1775** Virginians fight Governor Dunmore		
		Oct. 1775 Congress authorizes a navy			
		Nov. 1775 Congress appoints a committee to handle foreign affairs			

1776—Independence

WORLD EVENTS	TERRITORIAL EXPANSION	POLITICS	MILITARY	ECONOMICS and SCIENCE	RELIGION, ARTS and PEOPLE
1776 Adam Smith's *An Inquiry into the Nature and Causes of the Wealth of Nations* is published	**1776** Watauga settlements become part of North Carolina	**Apr.-May 1776** North Carolina and Virginia authorize delegations to vote for independence	**Feb.-June 1776** Tories fight patriots in the South	**c. 1776** Continuous highway system extends from Boston to South Carolina	**1776** Virginia *Bill of Rights* advocates "free exercise of religion"
1776-88 Edward Gibbon's *The Decline and Fall of the Roman Empire* appears	**1776** Kentucky settlements incorporated into Virginia	**June 7, 1776** Lee offers a resolution for independence	**Mar. 1776** British evacuate Boston	**1776** Congress sends Silas Deane to Europe to purchase war supplies	**1776** Phi Beta Kappa founded, at the College of William and Mary
		July 4, 1776 Congress adopts Declaration of Independence	**Apr.-July 1776** Americans retreat from Canada	**1776** Congress opens ports of colonies to trade of all nations except Britain	**1776-83** Thomas Paine writes "Common Sense," "Public Good," "The Crisis"
	1777 Cherokee Indians cede lands in the South	**Sept. 1776** Abortive peace conference held on Staten Island, New York	**Aug. 1776** British overwhelm colonials in battle of Long Island	**1776** Louis XVI of France subsidizes company to supply Americans with munitions	**1776-90** Anglican church disestablished in all colonies in which it had been tax-supported
		Sept. 1776 Congress appoints first diplomatic commission	**Sept. 1776** British occupy New York City; fire destroys much of town	**1776** American trade shifts to Holland, France, Spain	
		1776-77 Eleven states adopt new constitutions	**Oct. 1776** Arnold delays British at battle of Valcour Bay	**1776-81** New England, Middle States and Congress attempt to stabilize wages and prices	
			Oct. 1776 Washington eludes Howe at battle of White Plains	**1776-83** Revolution produces a business boom and inflation	
			Nov.-Dec. 1776 Americans retreat across New Jersey	**1776-83** Entail and primogeniture virtually abolished by state legislation	
		June 1777 Congress adopts the "Stars and Stripes"	**Dec. 1776** Washington wins at Trenton	**1776-87** Slave trade prohibited or heavily taxed in most of the states	
		Sept.-Dec. 1777 Attempt to discredit Washington by Conway Cabal	**Jan. 1777** Washington wins at Princeton	**c. 1777-78** Oliver Evans invents machine to speed wool production	**1777-82** Gilbert Stuart studies painting in London and achieves success
		Dec. 1777 France recognizes U.S. independence	**1777** Lafayette and other foreign officers enter American army	**1777-82** States appropriate Loyalist property	
1778 Captain John Cook discovers Sandwich Islands, later known as Hawaii	**1778** George Rogers Clark founds Louisville		**Oct. 1777** British defeat at Saratoga ends major campaign		**1778** Jonathan Carver's book *Travels Through the Interior Parts of North America* appears
	1778 Maryland refuses to ratify Articles of Confederation until all states cede their western lands to Congress		**Winter 1777-78** Ordeal of Valley Forge		**1778** Francis Hopkinson writes satirical poem "The Battle of the Kegs"
			July 1778 Clark captures Kaskaskia		
			July-Nov. 1778 Wyoming and Cherry Valley massacres		
			Dec. 1778 Savannah falls to British		
1778 France declares war on England			**Jan.-June 1779** British move north from Savannah		
			May-Sept. 1779 British and Americans clash in skirmishes around New York		
			Sept. 1779 *Bonhomme Richard* beats *Serapis*		

1779 Thomas Jefferson fails to achieve passage by Virginia legislature of his bill providing for first modern public school system
1779-90 Chancellor George Wythe offers first law lectures at the College of William and Mary
1780 The first Universalist church in the U.S. built in Gloucester, Massachusetts

1778 First American pharmacopoeia published, by William Brown
1780 Inflation sweeps country, Continental currency falls in value
1780 John Adams helps found American Academy of Arts and Sciences in Boston

Sept.-Oct. 1779 Americans, despite French naval aid, fail at Savannah
May 1780 Washington's troops mutiny at Morristown
July 1780 French reach Newport
Aug. 1780 Americans lose at Camden
Sept. 1780 Treason of Benedict Arnold exposed
Oct. 1780 Americans win at King's Mountain
Dec. 1780-Sept. 1781 Greene outmaneuvers British in Carolinas and draws them into Virginia

Feb. 1778 Franco-American alliance formed
Apr. 1778 English belatedly send Carlisle Peace Commission to forestall U.S. ratification of French alliance
Aug. 1779 Congress begins debate on peace terms
Sept. 1779 John Jay appointed to negotiate Spanish recognition and alliance

1779 Spain enters the war against England
1779-83 Spain and France unsuccessfully lay siege to Gibraltar
1780 Russia forms League of Armed Neutrality
1780 England declares war on Holland
1780-85 Joseph II reigns as king of Austria

1779 onward: Migration over Wilderness Trail into Kentucky and Tennessee resumed
1780 New York and Connecticut cede to U.S., their western land claims

1781—Confederation

1782 Crevecoeur writes *Letters from an American Farmer*
1782-83 Thomas Jefferson writes *Notes on the State of Virginia*
1783 Noah Webster publishes *The American Spelling Book*
1784 John Filson writes his *Discovery, Settlement, and Present State of Kentucke*
1784 First theological seminary in U.S. opens

1785 Madison's "Memorial and Remonstrance against Religious Assessments"
1785 University of Georgia, first state university, chartered
1785-92 Painter John Trumbull records Revolutionary scenes
1786 The Stoughton (Massachusetts) Musical Society, still in existence, organized
1786 *Pittsburgh Gazette*, first newspaper west of the Appalachians, appears

1781 Robert Morris appointed Superintendent of Finance and struggles to supply army
1783 Dutch loan aids hard-pressed U.S. Treasury
1783 Harvard Medical School opens
1783 Franklin invents bifocal glasses
1783 onward: Britain restricts U.S. trade with West Indies
1783-89 Trade unions grow; strikes increase
1784 U.S. enters China trade
1784-87 Economic depression; states move to alleviate national scarcity of specie
1784-89 Imports from Britain climb close to prewar level; U.S. exports reach 50 per cent of prewar level
1785 Potomac Company plans canal system to West
1785 Oliver Evans perfects automatic flour mill
1785 National coinage established by law
1786 Dr. Benjamin Rush opens first free dispensary, in Philadelphia

Jan. 1781 Pennsylvania troops mutiny
Apr. 1781 Captain John Barry captures *Mars* and *Minerva* from British
May 1781 Washington and Rochambeau plan joint Franco-American campaign
May-Oct. 1781 Cornwallis campaigns through Virginia
Sept. 1781 British fleet forced to withdraw at Yorktown
Oct. 19, 1781 British army surrenders at Yorktown
June 1783 American army disbands without authority: Congress flees Philadelphia to escape discontented soldiers
Nov. 1783 British evacuate New York City
Dec. 1783 Washington says farewell to his officers
May-July 1784 Pennsylvania and Connecticut citizens clash over Wyoming Valley claims

Mar. 1781 Articles of Confederation ratified
June 1781 Congress appoints peace commission
Apr. 1782 Peace talks begin in Paris
Sept. 1782 Start of formal peace negotiations
Apr. 1783 Loyalists sail from New York
Sept. 3, 1783 Americans and British sign final peace: France and Spain sign separate peace with England
May 1784 John Jay appointed Secretary of Foreign Affairs
Dec. 1784 Congress votes plans for permanent federal capital and designates New York temporary capital

Feb.-Mar. 1785 Congress appoints ministers to Britain and France
Mar. 1785 Congress appoints Henry Knox Secretary of War
Jan. 1786 Virginia adopts Statute for Religious Freedom
June 1786 Treaty with Morocco protecting U.S. commerce
Aug. 1786 Proposal submitted to Congress to revise Articles of Confederation
Aug. 1786-Feb. 1787 Shays's Rebellion
Sept. 1786 Annapolis Convention held

1781 Holy Roman Empire joins League of Armed Neutrality
1782 Holland recognizes American independence
1782 Lord North resigns English ministry; succeeded by Rockingham; then Shelburne takes over
1782 Portugal and Prussia join League of Armed Neutrality
1783 Lord North and Charles James Fox head coalition ministry in England
1783 England, France, Spain and U.S. make peace at Paris
1783-1801 William Pitt's first ministry
1784 England and Holland conclude final peace
1786-97 Frederick William II rules Prussia

1782 Congress upholds Pennsylvania's claim to lands disputed by Connecticut
1784 Congress adopts Land Ordinance to organize territories for statehood
1784 Virginia cedes western land claims to U.S.
1784 Iroquois sign treaty ceding all lands west of Niagara River to U.S.
1784-87 Independent State of Franklin, made up of parts of Tennessee and Virginia, seeks admission to Union
1785 Indian tribes cede Ohio lands to U.S.
1785 Land Ordinance provides methods of sale of public lands
1785 Massachusetts cedes its Great Lakes land claims to U.S.
1786 Massachusetts and New York settle conflicting western land claims
1786 Connecticut cedes part of its western land claims to U.S.

1787—Constitution

1787 *The Contrast*, by Royall Turner, first American comedy to be produced professionally, is performed in New York

1789 Protestant Episcopal Church organized in Philadelphia
1789 First American novel, *The Power of Sympathy*, by William Hill Brown, published

1787 Slavery prohibited in Northwest Territory
1787 Noncondensing, high-pressure steam engine patented by Oliver Evans in Maryland
1787 John Fitch's steamboat launched on Delaware
1787-90 Captain Robert Gray opens fur trade by sea from New England to Pacific Northwest to China and back
1788 Dissection of human cadavers provokes serious rioting in New York City

Feb.-May 1787 Delegates named to Philadelphia Convention
May 1787 Constitutional Convention opened
Aug.-Sept. 1787 Congress debates various proposals
Sept. 1787 State delegations vote final approval of draft Constitution
Sept. 1787 Congress asks for state ratifying conventions
Dec. 1787-Aug. 1788 State ratifying conventions adopt the Constitution
1787-88 Hamilton, Madison and Jay write *The Federalist* papers

1787-92 Russia and Austria fight Turkey
1788 French Estates-General summoned
1788-1808 Charles IV reigns in Spain
1789 French Revolution starts

1787 Northwest Ordinance adopted
1787 South Carolina cedes western lands to U.S.

FOR FURTHER READING

These books were selected for their interest and authority in the preparation of this volume, and for their usefulness to readers seeking additional information on specific points. An asterisk (*) marks works available in both hard-cover and paperback editions; a dagger (†) indicates availability only in paperback.

GENERAL READING

Andrews, Charles M., *The Colonial Period of American History* (4 vols.). Yale University Press, 1934-1938.

Bailey, Thomas A., *A Diplomatic History of the American People.* Appleton-Century-Crofts, 1958.

Carman, Harry J., Harold C. Syrett and Bernard W. Wishy, *A History of the American People* (Vol. I). Alfred A. Knopf, 1960.

Freeman, Douglas Southall, *George Washington* (7 vols., Vol. 7 by Carroll, John A., and Mary W. Ashworth). Scribner's, 1948-1957.

Hofstadter, Richard, William Miller and Daniel Aaron, *The American Republic* (Vol. I). Prentice-Hall, 1959.

Malone, Dumas and Basil Rauch, *Empire for Liberty* (Vol. I). Appleton-Century-Crofts, 1960.

Morison, Samuel Eliot and Henry Steele Commager, *The Growth of the American Republic* (Vol. I). Oxford University Press, 1962.

†Rossiter, Clinton L., *The First American Revolution.* Harcourt, Brace & World, 1956.

Wertenbaker, Thomas J., *Founding of American Civilization: The Middle Colonies.* Scribner's, 1938.

*Wright, Louis B., *The Cultural Life of the American Colonies: 1607-1763.* Harper & Row, 1957.

THE AMERICAN REVOLUTION (CHAPTERS 1, 2, 3, 4)

Alden, John Richard, *The American Revolution: 1775-1783.* Harper & Row, 1954

*Becker, Carl, *The Declaration of Independence: A Study in the History of Political Ideas.* Alfred A. Knopf, 1942.

*Bemis, Samuel Flagg, *The Diplomacy of the American Revolution.* Peter Smith, 1958.

Bliven, Bruce, Jr., *Battle for Manhattan.* Holt, Rinehart & Winston, 1956.

Burnett, Edmund Cody, *The Continental Congress.* Macmillan, 1941.

Commager, Henry Steele, and Richard B. Morris, *The Spirit of 'Seventy-Six* (2 vols.). Bobbs-Merrill, 1958.

Corwin, Edward S., *French Policy and the American Alliance of 1778.* Shoe String Press, 1962.

Dumbauld, Edward, *Declaration of Independence and What It Means Today.* University of Oklahoma Press, 1950.

*Jameson, J. Franklin, *The American Revolution Considered as a Social Movement.* Peter Smith, 1961.

Malone, Dumas, *Jefferson the Virginian.* Little, Brown, 1948.

Malone, Dumas, Hirst Milhollen and Milton Kaplan, *The Story of the Declaration of Independence.* Oxford University Press, 1954.

Miller, John C., *Triumph of Freedom 1775-1783.* Little, Brown, 1948.

Montross, Lynn, *Rag, Tag and Bobtail.* Harper & Row, 1952. *The Reluctant Rebels.* Harper & Row, 1950.

*Peckham, Howard H., *The War for Independence. A Military History.* University of Chicago Press, 1958.

Plumb, John H., *The First Four Georges.* Macmillan, 1957.

*Scheer, George F., and Hugh F. Rankin, *Rebels and Redcoats.* World Publishing, 1957.

Trevelyan, George Otto, *The American Revolution* (4 vols.). Longmans, Green, 1905-1912. *George the Third and Charles Fox, the concluding part of The American Revolution.* (2 vols.). Longmans, Green, 1912-1914.

Tyler, Moses Coit, *The Literary History of the American Revolution* (2 vols.). Frederick Ungar, 1957.

Van Doren, Carl, *Benjamin Franklin: A Biography.* Viking Press, 1956. *Secret History of the American Revolution.* Viking Press, 1941.

Van Tyne, Claude H., *The Causes of the War of Independence.* Peter Smith, 1952. *The Loyalists in the American Revolution.* Peter Smith, 1929.

Wallace, Willard M., *Appeal to Arms,* Harper & Row, 1951.

Ward, Christopher, *The War of the Revolution* (2 vols.). Macmillan, 1952.

CONFEDERATION AND CONSTITUTION (CHAPTERS 5, 6)

Aaron, Daniel (ed.), *America in Crisis.* Alfred A. Knopf, 1952.

*Beard, Charles A., *An Economic Interpretation of the Constitution of the United States.* Macmillan, 1935.

Bemis, Samuel Flagg (ed.), *The American Secretaries of State and Their Diplomacy* (Vol. I). Alfred A. Knopf, 1927.

Beveridge, Albert J., *The Life of John Marshall* (Vol. I). Houghton Mifflin, 1939.

Brant, Irving, *James Madison* (Vol. III, *Father of the Constitution*). Bobbs-Merrill, 1950.

Brown, Robert E., *Charles Beard and the Constitution.* Princeton University Press, 1956.

*Farrand, Max, *The Framing of the Constitution of the United States.* Yale University Press, 1913.

Fiske, John, *The Critical Period of American History, 1783-1789.* Houghton Mifflin, 1957.

Fitzpatrick, John C., *George Washington Himself.* Bobbs-Merrill, 1933.

*Jensen, Merrill, *The Articles of Confederation.* University of Wisconsin Press, 1959. *The New Nation.* Alfred A. Knopf, 1950.

McDonald, Forrest, *We the People. The Economic Origins of the Constitution.* University of Chicago Press, 1958.

*McLaughlin, Andrew C., *The Confederation and the Constitution, 1783-1789.* Harper & Row, 1905.

Monaghan, Frank, *John Jay, Defender of Liberty.* Bobbs-Merrill, 1935.

Morris, Richard B. (ed.), *Alexander Hamilton and the Founding of the Nation.* Dial Press, 1957.

Nevins, Allan, *The American States during and after the Revolution, 1775-1789.* Macmillan, 1924.

Schuyler, Robert L., *The Constitution of the United States: An Historical Survey of its Formation.* Peter Smith, 1952.

Smith, C. Page, *James Wilson: Founding Father, 1742-1798.* University of North Carolina Press, 1956.

Stephenson, Nathaniel W., and Waldo H. Dunn, *George Washington* (2 vols.). Oxford University Press, 1940.

Tebbel, John, *George Washington's America.* E. P. Dutton, 1954.

*Van Doren, Carl, *The Great Rehearsal.* Viking Press, 1948.

Warren, Charles, *The Making of the Constitution.* Harvard University Press, 1947.

ACKNOWLEDGMENTS

The editors of this book are particularly indebted to the following persons and institutions: Virginia Daikers, Milton Kaplan and Carl Stange, Library of Congress, Washington, D.C.; Captain Wade de Weese, United States Naval Academy Museum, Annapolis, Maryland; Elizabeth Roth, New York Public Library Print Collection; the staff of Mount Vernon; J. A. Lloyd Hyde, New York, New York; Ted C. Sowers, Morristown National Historical Park; Susie Hallberg, Chamber of Commerce, Fredericksburg, Virginia; Ann Parrish, Kenmore House, Fredericksburg, Virginia; and Marguerite H. Munson and Judy Higgins.

PICTURE CREDITS

The sources for the illustrations in this book are shown below. Credits for pictures from left to right are separated by semicolons, top to bottom by dashes. Sources have been abbreviated as follows: Bettmann—The Bettmann Archive; Brown—Brown Brothers; Culver—Culver Pictures; LC—Library of Congress; Metropolitan—The Metropolitan Museum of Art, N.Y.C.; N-YHS—The New-York Historical Society, N.Y.C.; NYPL—The New York Public Library; N.Y. State Hist. Assn.—New York State Historical Association, Cooperstown.

CHAPTER I: 6—Arnold Newman, courtesy Joe Kindig Jr., Harold L. Peterson Fort Ticonderoga Museum, National Park Service, Pennsylvania Farm Museum of Landis Valley. 9—Bettmann. 10, 11—Culver except bottom left N. Y. State Hist. Assn. 15—Sy Seidman. 16, 17—American Philosophical Society; Official U. S. Army photo. 18, 19—N. Y. State Hist. Assn.; Fernand Bourges, courtesy of Gilbert Darlington Collection. 20, 21—Fernand Bourges, courtesy Connecticut Historical Society, Hartford—Culver. 22, 23—Henry B. Beville, *Burning of Charles Town* (artist unknown), National Gallery of Art, Washington, D.C. From the collection of American Primitive Paintings given by Edgar William and Bernice Chrysler Garbisch. 24—Fernand Bourges, painting in the Fort Ticonderoga Museum, Fort Ticonderoga, N. Y. 25—Museum of Fine Arts, Boston, courtesy American Heritage Publishing Co., Inc.—N-YHS. 26, 27—Courtesy Harry Shaw Newman, The Old Print Shop, N.Y.C.; Fernand Bourges, Yale University Art Gallery. 28, 29—Courtesy William H. Duncan and Colonial Williamsburg—courtesy Morristown National Historical Park, Morristown, N. J., and American Heritage Publishing Co., Inc. 30, 31—Culver; Fernand Bourges, courtesy Emmet Collection—NYPL (Manuscript Division).

CHAPTER II: 32—Andreas Feininger, courtesy Adams National Historic Site, Ancient and Honorable Artillery Company, Boston Athenaeum, Bostonian Society, collection of Mrs. Nina Fletcher Little, Massachusetts Historical Society. 34, 35 —From *The Pictorial Field-Book of the Revolution*, Vol. II, Harper, 1855; Visual Discoveries, Inc. 39—Bottom: The Free Library of Philadelphia. 40, 41—Culver; N. Y. State Hist. Assn.—NYPL; Bettmann. 42, 43—Herbert Orth; Kennedy Galleries, Inc. 44—Herbert Orth, courtesy of Lafayette College, donor Allan P. Kirby. 45—Top left: Culver; right: Herbert Orth, State House, Annapolis, Md. 46—Herbert Orth, courtesy City of Boston, on loan to Museum of Fine Arts, Boston—Andreas Feininger, courtesy of the Adams National Historic Site, National Park Service, Department of the Interior. 47—Courtesy Harvard University. 48, 49—Herbert Orth, courtesy Mrs. T. Charlton Henry (2); Herbert Orth, courtesy of Princeton University—courtesy Princeton University Library. 50—Herbert Orth, from the collections of The Historical Society of Pennsylvania—Herbert Orth, courtesy of The Pennsylvania Academy of the Fine Arts. 51—Yale University Art Gallery. 52, 53— Top: Yale University Art Gallery.

CHAPTER III: 54—Herbert Orth, Yale University Art Gallery. 57, 58—Culver. 60, 61—Culver; N.Y. State Hist. Assn.—N.Y. State Hist. Assn.; Brown. 62, 63—Brown; N. Y. State Hist. Assn.—Culver—Essex Institute, Salem, Mass. 65—Sy Seidman. 66, 67—N.Y. State Hist. Assn.; Fernand Bourges, courtesy Fort Ticonderoga Museum, Fort Ticonderoga, N. Y. 68, 69—Fernand Bourges, courtesy Mrs. Nina Fletcher Little; courtesy Harry Shaw Newman, The Old Print Shop, N.Y.C.— Fernand Bourges, courtesy The Historical Society of Pennsylvania. 70, 71—Fernand Bourges, courtesy Fort Ticonderoga Museum, Fort Ticonderoga, N. Y.— Culver; courtesy Yale University Art Gallery and American Heritage Publishing Co., Inc. 72—N. Y. State Hist. Assn.—courtesy TIME and Metropolitan, the bequest of Charles Allen Munn, 1924. 73—Culver. 74, 75—The Valley Forge Historical Society, courtesy American Heritage Publishing Co., Inc.; collection of Gordon Abbott, Jr., courtesy American Heritage Publishing Co., Inc. 76, 77—The John Carter Brown Library, Brown University, courtesy American Heritage Publishing Co., Inc.; Jahn and Ollier Engraving Co., original painting in the Chicago Histori-

cal Society. 78, 79—Fernand Bourges, courtesy of the Monmouth County Historical Association.

CHAPTER IV: 80—Henry B. Beville, courtesy Henry Francis du Pont Winterthur Museum. 82—N. Y. State Hist. Assn. 84, 85—N. Y. State Hist. Assn. except bottom Culver. 86—Culver—N. Y. State Hist. Assn. 88—Courtesy British Museum, London. 89—Culver—From *The First Four Georges* by J. H. Plumb, published by B. T. Batsford Ltd., London (The Macmillan Company, N.Y.) courtesy American Heritage Publishing Co., Inc. 90, 91—The Mariners Museum, Newport News, Va.; Fernand Bourges, courtesy U. S. Naval Academy Museum. 92—The Mariners Museum, Newport News, Va. 93—Fernand Bourges, courtesy U. S. Naval Academy Museum—Independence National Historical Park, Philadelphia; Robert L. Harley, courtesy George A. Hopkins and the Massachusetts Historical Society— courtesy American Heritage Publishing Co., Inc.; Independence National Historical Park, Philadelphia. 94, 95—Courtesy the Honorable Joseph C. Duke, Sergeant-At-Arms, U.S. Senate and American Heritage Publishing Co., Inc. 96, 97—LC; Herbert Orth, courtesy Fordham University—Herbert Orth, NYPL. 98, 99—*Combat de la Chesapeake* by Theodore Gudin, Musée de Versailles, Numéro MV1433, courtesy American Heritage Publishing Co., Inc.—James Kincaid; Herbert Orth, courtesy U. S. Naval Academy Museum; National Maritime Museum, Greenwich Hospital Collection, courtesy American Heritage Publishing Co., Inc. 100, 101—Walter A. Curtin, *British Surrender at Yorktown* by Von Blarenberghe, courtesy Musée de Versailles, Numéro MV2265.

CHAPTER V: 102—Eric Schaal, courtesy Art Commission of the City of New York. 104—Culver. 105—Courtesy Emmet Collection-NYPL (Manuscript Division). 106, 107—Brown; Culver. 108, 109—Culver; NYPL. 112, 113—Bettmann; Culver —N. Y. State Hist. Assn.; Bettmann. 114, 115—Culver. 116,117—Culver—courtesy Historical and Philosophical Society of Ohio, Cincinnati; NYPL. 118, 119—LC; Bettmann—courtesy Carnegie Library at Pittsburgh and American Heritage Publishing Co., Inc. 120, 121—Culver. 122, 123—Left: Missouri Historical Society; bottom right Culver. 124, 125—Herbert Orth, courtesy Dr. Gray H. Twombly. 126, 127—Culver.

CHAPTER VI: 128—Sidney Farnsworth, The Cleveland Museum of Art, Hinman B. Hurlbut Collection. 130, 131—Bettmann—Culver. 132, 133—Sy Seidman, Culver. 134—Courtesy of C. P. Means, Charleston, S.C.—N. Y. State Hist. Assn. 135— Brown. 136—Culver—LC. 137—Brown. 138—N. Y. State Hist. Assn. 139—Nina Leen, courtesy The Mount Vernon Ladies' Association of The Union, Mount Vernon, Va. 140, 141—Nina Leen, courtesy Mrs. T. M. Heflin Sr., Fredericksburg, Va.; Nina Leen, courtesy The Home of Mary Washington owned and operated by the Association for the Preservation of Virginia Antiquities, Fredericksburg, Va. 142, 143—Nina Leen, courtesy The Mount Vernon Ladies' Association of The Union, Mount Vernon, Va. 144, 145—Nina Leen, courtesy The Mount Vernon Ladies' Association of The Union, Mount Vernon, Va. 146—Nina Leen, courtesy The Connecticut Society of the Colonial Dames of America—Nina Leen, picture through the courtesy and cooperation of the National Park Service, Morristown National Historical Park, Morristown, N. J. 147—Nina Leen, courtesy of the Sons of the Revolution in the State of New York, Headquarters, Fraunces Tavern, N. Y. C. 148, 149—Nina Leen, courtesy The Mount Vernon Ladies' Association of The Union, Mount Vernon, Va. 150, 151—Nina Leen, courtesy The Mount Vernon Ladies' Association of The Union, Mount Vernon, Va.

INDEX

This symbol in front of a page number indicates a photograph or painting of the subject mentioned.

Printed in U.S.A.

Ref
973
LIF

Morris, Richard B.
The making of a
nation

DATE DUE	

Ref
973
LIF

Morris, Richard B.
The making of a
nation

DATE DUE	BORROWER'S NAME	
	Sterioff	112
NOV 23 78	my B	AN
2-80	Wilson	
JAN 27 82	OXAN	2

For Reference

Not to be taken from this room